At Issue

I High School Dropouts

Other Books in the At Issue Series:

Alcohol Abuse

Animal Experimentation

Are Adoption Policies Fair?

Are Books Becoming Extinct?

Biofuels

Cancer

Child Pornography

Distracted Driving

Embryonic and Adult Stem Cells

Gay Marriage

Health Care Legislation

Mexico's Drug War

Reality TV

Tasers

The US Energy Grid

What Is the Impact of Twitter?

At Issue

I High School Dropouts

Judeen Bartos, Book Editor

GREENHAVEN PRESS
A part of Gale, Cengage Learning

GALE
CENGAGE Learning·

Detroit • New York • San Francisco • New Haven, Conn • Waterville, Maine • London

Elizabeth Des Chenes, *Director, Publishing Solutions*

© 2013 Greenhaven Press, a part of Gale, Cengage Learning

Gale and Greenhaven Press are registered trademarks used herein under license.

For more information, contact:
Greenhaven Press
27500 Drake Rd.
Farmington Hills, MI 48331-3535
Or you can visit our Internet site at gale.cengage.com

For product information and technology assistance, contact us at

Gale Customer Support, 1-800-877-4253
For permission to use material from this text or product, submit all requests online at www.cengage.com/permissions

Further permissions questions can be emailed to permissionrequest@cengage.com

Articles in Greenhaven Press anthologies are often edited for length to meet page requirements. In addition, original titles of these works are changed to clearly present the main thesis and to explicitly indicate the author's opinion. Every effort is made to ensure that Greenhaven Press accurately reflects the original intent of the authors. Every effort has been made to trace the owners of copyrighted material.

Cover image © Images.com/Corbis.

LIBRARY OF CONGRESS CATALOGING-IN-PUBLICATION DATA

High school dropouts / Judeen Bartos, book editor.
   p. cm. -- (At issue)
   Includes bibliographical references and index.
   ISBN 978-0-7377-6181-8 (hardcover) -- ISBN 978-0-7377-6182-5 (pbk.)
   1. High school dropouts--United States--Juvenile literature. 2. Dropouts--United States--Juvenile literature. I. Bartos, Judeen.
   LC146.6.H54 2013
   371.2'9130973--dc23

                                2012045149

Printed in the United States of America
1 2 3 4 5   17 16 15 14 13

Contents

Introduction   7

1. High Dropout Rates Negatively Affect   10
   Students and the Nation
   Alliance for Excellent Education

2. Can Obama Reverse the Dropout Crisis?   16
   Richard Lee Colvin

3. Zero-Tolerance Policies Make It Harder   23
   for At-Risk Students to Graduate
   Beverly Ford

4. District Innovates to Address   31
   Dropout Problem
   Michelle R. Davis

5. New Report Shows Graduation Chasm   37
   for Black Males
   Jamelle Bouie

6. Latinas Are Hit Hard by the Dropout Problem   40
   Catherine Gewertz

7. Pregnant and Parenting Teens Require Special   45
   Support to Stay in School
   Laura Varlas

8. LGBTQ Students Need a Safe Alternative   52
   to Thrive and Stay in School
   Jorge Salazar

9. Engaging Entrepreneurial Students Is Critical   59
   to Keeping Them in School
   Sylvia Watts McKinney

10. How to Get High School Dropouts   63
    into "Recovery"?
    Stacy Teicher Khadaroo

11. Early Colleges Provide an Opportunity   70
    for At-Risk Students to Succeed
    Tamar Lewin

12. America Should Emulate Other Countries   76
    in Addressing the Dropout Crisis
    Nancy Hoffman

Organizations to Contact   89
Bibliography   94
Index   98

Introduction

High school dropouts have received increased attention in recent years as the number of dropouts in the United States has remained persistently high. Students who drop out face a host of risks and repercussions throughout their lives, and society as a whole is poorly served by having a high number of undereducated citizens. Opinions are plentiful on how to fix the problem and help more students stay in school, graduate, and move on to college.

Many reformers have focused on the issue of standardized tests, which have assumed ever greater importance in assessing the success of students and teachers. Federal initiatives such as the No Child Left Behind Act of 2001 and the Race to the Top program launched in 2010 seek to reward schools that perform and punish those that do not; one key measure for this performance is standardized test scores. Entrance into college is largely dependent on test results as well. With so much riding on test scores, the pressure proves daunting for many students, who feel they cannot compete in this environment and instead choose to drop out.

Examining this high-stakes educational competition, some question whether the price is too high, when so many students are left behind under the current system. Steve Denning, who writes on leadership for *Forbes* magazine, is one expert who has offered a diagnosis of the problem. Denning asserts that the issue with K-12 education is that it is based on a factory model of management. This methodology, which is applied in the majority of school districts in the United States, puts the needs of the system above the needs of those who are in it. The burden to adapt is placed on the students and their families, teachers, and school officials. Reformers point out that while this model of management has repeatedly been proven to be ineffective in the industrial world, schools continue to cling to it with negative consequences.

Denning believes the intense focus on student education as a product, similar to a product assembled in a factory, has a harmful effect on students. It does not help them become adults who will flourish and be lifelong learners. Denning asserts, in a September 1, 2011, column in *Forbes*, that the single most important reform that can take place in K-12 education requires a shift in focus: "The goal needs to shift from one of making a system that teaches children a curriculum more efficiently to one of making the system more effective by inspiring lifelong learning in students, so that they are able to have full and productive lives in a rapidly shifting economy."

Denning is not alone in his views. "Community schools" have become a nationwide movement that stand in contrast to the predominant educational model. David L. Kirp, writing in *The Nation* on May 27, 2010, provides this description: "These schools break the traditional six-and-a-half-hour day, 180-days-a-year mold, with programs before and after school, as well as weekends and during the summer. They supplement academics with medical care and social services. They involve parents as learners and teachers. And they partner with high-asset city agencies, community groups, and businesses, attracting new funds to the schools while connecting students to the universe beyond the schoolhouse door."

Community schools recognize that academics do not happen within a vacuum. If a student's basic needs are not being met, it is difficult to succeed in school. These schools, located in areas of high need, can change the course of children's lives and increase the possibility that students will stay in school and avoid risks in their lives as they mature. "The research shows that at topnotch community schools fewer students are suspended and fewer drop out. The achievement gap shrinks, and more youngsters go to college," says Kirp.

While these models are a bright spot in the battle to keep students in school and on a path to graduation, they have proven to be difficult to replicate on a large scale. Unlike businesses that can take a successful model and expand it, schools are more organic in nature, requiring local leadership and effort at the grassroots level in order to succeed. The Bill and Melinda Gates Foundation is one philanthropic organization that has found this to be true. In the last ten years the foundation has tackled the challenge of reducing the number of high school dropouts and increasing college readiness. But its reform efforts have had mixed results. According to Amanda Paulson, writing for the *Christian Science Monitor* in January 2010, "The Gates Foundation has invested more than $1 billion in improving US high schools, with both noteworthy successes and a number of false starts." Even among the positive results, replication has proven difficult to attain.

A growing body of evidence suggests that the high-pressure, high-stakes atmosphere of most schools today does more harm than good and can indeed lead to more students deciding to drop out. While rigor and high expectations are important components of any education, the message of how to succeed has been undermined. "Children will race to the top when they discover passion and purpose from the inside, not because of extrinsic rewards like test scores, grades, or trophies," says Marilyn Price-Mitchell in a September 2011 article in *Psychology Today*. "What matters most to families and to our democracy is that children develop into caring, productive young adults who critically think about and actively engage in the world around them," suggests Price-Mitchell.

The contributors to *At Issue: High School Dropouts* examine many aspects of the American educational system, assessing the reasons why students drop out of school, the unique needs and challenges of different students, and potential solutions to the problem.

1

High Dropout Rates Negatively Affect Students and the Nation

Alliance for Excellent Education

The Alliance for Excellent Education is a Washington, DC-based national policy and advocacy organization that works to improve education policy in America.

America pays dearly for its high school dropouts. When young people do not graduate from high school the economic impact is extensive. For the dropout, wages remain significantly lower throughout their lives. The country's overall economy is weakened by their diminished purchasing power. Socially, the consequences are also significant. High school graduates have a much more positive social prognosis—their health is better, they are less likely to commit crimes or utilize government assistance programs, and perhaps most importantly, they are able to raise a healthier and better-educated future generation of children. The cost of high school dropouts is immense and every effort should be made to change current trends.

Every school day, nearly 7,000 students become dropouts. Annually, that adds up to about 1.2 million students who will not graduate from high school with their peers as scheduled. Lacking a high school diploma, these individuals will be far more likely than graduates to spend their lives periodically unemployed, on government assistance, or cycling in and out of the prison system.

Most high school dropouts see the result of their decision to leave school very clearly in the slimness of their wallets. The average annual income for a high school dropout in 2009 was $19,540, compared to $27,380 for a high school graduate, a difference of $7,840. The impact on the country's economy is less visible, but cumulatively its effect is staggering.

Not only do employed high school dropouts earn less than employed high school graduates, high school dropouts are much more likely to be unemployed during economic downturns.

If the nation's secondary schools improved sufficiently to graduate all of their students, rather than the 72 percent of students who currently graduate annually, the payoff would be significant. For instance, if the students who dropped out of the Class of 2011 had graduated, the nation's economy would likely benefit from nearly $154 billion in additional income over the course of their lifetimes.

Everyone benefits from increased graduation rates. The graduates themselves, on average, will earn higher wages and enjoy more comfortable and secure lifestyles. At the same time, the nation benefits from their increased purchasing power, collects higher tax receipts, and sees higher levels of worker productivity.

An Economic Recession Is More Likely to Impact High School Dropouts

Not only do employed high school dropouts earn less than employed high school graduates, high school dropouts are much more likely to be unemployed during economic downturns. Since the economic recession began in December 2007, the national unemployment rate has gone from 5 percent to 9.1 percent in August 2011. . . .

The unemployment rate for individuals of all education levels has skyrocketed since December 2007, but high school dropouts have faced the most difficulty with finding a job. According to data from the U.S. Bureau of Labor Statistics, the unemployment rate for high school dropouts in August 2011—four years after the start of the recession—was 14.3 percent, compared to 9.6 percent for high school graduates, 8.2 percent for individuals with some college credits or an associate's degree, and 4.3 percent for individuals with a bachelor's degree or higher.

Higher Levels of Education Translate into Higher Earnings

Recent research conducted by the Alliance for Excellent Education in partnership with Economic Modeling Specialists, Inc., an Idaho-based economic modeling firm, provides a look at the additional earnings an individual would likely expect over the course of his or her lifetime by completing high school. This analysis is based upon state-specific economic data that reflects the postrecession economic reality.

Dropouts represent a tremendous loss of human potential and productivity, and they significantly reduce the nation's ability to compete in an increasingly global economy.

The calculations . . . show the monetary benefits each state would likely accrue over the lifetimes of just one year's worth of dropouts if those students had graduated. Calculations are based on the number of dropouts and average earnings by education level, which causes the numbers to vary from state to state: Vermont (at the low end) would likely see its economy increase by $147 million; Massachusetts (near the middle) would likely add $2 billion to its economy, and California's economy (at the high end) would likely accrue an additional $21 billion over the lifetimes of just one year's worth of dropouts if those students had graduated. These figures are conservative and do not take into account the added economic growth generated from each new dollar put into the economy.

All told, these additional earnings from a single high school class would likely pour a total of $154 billion into the national economy. Unless high schools are able to graduate their students at higher rates, nearly 12 million students will likely drop out over the next decade, resulting in a loss to the nation of *$1.5 trillion.*

Society Benefits from an Increase in High School Graduates

Obviously, dropouts are a drain on the nation's economy and the economies of each state. Lower local, state, and national tax revenues are the most obvious consequence of higher dropout rates; even when dropouts are employed, they earn significantly lower wages than do graduates. State and local economies suffer further when they have less-educated populaces, as they find it more difficult to attract new business investment. Simultaneously, these entities must spend more on social programs when their populations have lower educational levels.

The nation's economy and competitive standing also suffer when there are high dropout rates. Among developed countries, the United States ranks twenty-first in high school graduation rates and fifteenth in college attainment rates among twenty-five- to thirty-four-year-olds. Dropouts represent a tremendous loss of human potential and productivity, and they significantly reduce the nation's ability to compete in an increasingly global economy. Furthermore, recent estimates project that the future domestic workforce demands will require higher levels of education among U.S. workers. However, without significant improvements in the high school and postsecondary completion rates, the nation is on track to fall short by up to 3 million postsecondary degrees by 2018.

The nation can no longer afford to have more than one-quarter of its students leave high school without a diploma.

High school graduates, on the other hand, provide both economic and social benefits to society. In addition to earning higher wages—resulting in corresponding benefits to local, state, and national economic conditions—high school graduates live longer, are less likely to be teen parents, and are more likely to raise healthier, better-educated children. In fact, children of parents who graduate from high school are far more likely to graduate from high school, compared to children of parents without high school degrees. High school graduates are also less likely to commit crimes, rely on government health care, or use other public services such as food stamps or housing assistance. Additionally, high school graduates engage in civic activity, including voting and volunteering in their communities, and at higher levels.

Improving High Schools Would Help Reduce the Dropout Rate

To increase the number of students who graduate from high school, the nation's secondary schools must address the reasons why most students drop out. In a recent survey of high school dropouts, respondents indicated that they felt alienated at school and that no one noticed if they failed to show up for class. High school dropouts also complained that school did not reflect real-world challenges. More than half of the respondents said that the major reason for dropping out of high school was that they felt their classes were uninteresting and irrelevant.

Others leave because they are not doing well academically. According to the 2009 National Assessment of Educational Progress in reading, only about 30 percent of entering high school freshmen read proficiently, which generally means that as the material in their textbooks becomes more challenging, they drop even further behind.

The nation can no longer afford to have more than one-quarter of its students leave high school without a diploma. High schools must be improved to give all students the excellent education that will prepare them for college and a career, and to be productive members of society.

2

Can Obama Reverse the Dropout Crisis?

Richard Lee Colvin

Richard Lee Colvin, a longtime journalist, is director of the Hechinger Institute on Education and the Media, Teachers College, Columbia University, and editor of The Hechinger Report, *an independent, foundation-supported news operation based at Teachers College. Beginning in 2013,* The Hechinger Report, *at www.hechingerreport.org, will provide ongoing coverage of the dropout crisis in America and how the nation can increase the high school graduation rate.*

America's dropout problem is often viewed as chronic and irreversible. Economic difficulties negatively affect dropout rates and leave a future generation undereducated and less able to compete in the jobs market. The nation as a whole is negatively affected by high dropout rates. President Barack Obama has made the dropout problem a major priority of his administration and has offered funding to encourage poor-performing schools to make changes.

In his first address to Congress in February 2009, when the nation teetered on the brink of economic collapse, President Obama declared that "dropping out of high school is no longer an option. It's not just quitting on yourself, it's quitting on your country—and this country needs and values the talents of every American." Since then, the administration has

Richard Lee Colvin, "Can Obama reverse the dropout crisis?" *Washington Monthly*, Volume 42, Issue 7-8, July/August 2010. Copyright 2010 © by Washington Monthly. All rights reserved. Reproduced by permission.

made a major commitment to increasing America's high school graduation rate, which was once the highest in the developed world and is now among the lowest. Leading researchers now agree that 25 to 30 percent of students who enroll in American high schools fail to graduate. In many of the country's largest urban school districts, such as Detroit, Cleveland, and Indianapolis, the dropout rate is as high as 60 percent, and rates are similarly high in many rural areas. A generation ago, high school dropouts could still join the military, or get work on assembly lines, and had a fair chance of finding their way in the world. President Obama does not exaggerate when he implies that today's America has little use for dropouts and cannot expect to flourish so long as their numbers remain so high.

The administration has proposed nearly $1 billion in its latest budget specifically for the dropout problem. And it has already put $7.4 billion on the table, including its famous Race to the Top grants, which states and districts can get only if they agree to overhaul their worst-performing high schools. These are the 2,000 or so high schools that Obama and Secretary of Education Arne Duncan refer to as "dropout factories"—schools that graduate fewer than 60 percent of their students and account for more than half the nation's dropouts.

This level of financial commitment to fixing America's underperforming high schools is unprecedented. The 1983 Nation at Risk report, which marked the start of the modern era of education reform, did not so much as mention the dropout problem even as it called for higher graduation requirements. Between 1988 and 1995, only eighty-nine school districts won federal grants for dropout prevention programs. The No Child Left Behind Act of 2002 applied mostly to grades three through eight. While it nominally required states to hold high schools accountable for dropout rates, it ended up allowing them to lowball the problem. Generally, the thought among educational reformers has been to concentrate on preschool and grade school education, and hope that success there would result in better student performance in high school.

Informing this approach was a not-unreasonable fear that by the time struggling students reached high school, there was little that could be done to turn them around. A 1999 report found that what few federally financed attempts had been made to improve teaching in high schools did not lower the dropout rate. A 2002 General Accounting Office report summed up twenty years of federal dropout prevention efforts by noting that the few that had been rigorously evaluated showed mixed results. Worse, even the occasional success stories were not replicated.

Which leaves a big question: Do we know enough today to make good use of a new massive federal commitment to lowering the dropout rate? One reason to think so is that there has been a data-driven revolution in our understanding of the problem.

During the 1970s and '80s and well into the '90s, educators and social scientists attempted, without a lot of success, to discover the most important predictors of whether a student would drop out or not. Mostly they wound up using known risk factors—such as extreme poverty, poor grades, and contact with the juvenile justice and foster care systems—to predict who would drop out and try, through mentoring and other services, to keep them from doing so. Students who fit those categories were on average more likely to drop out. But averages can be misleading, especially when there is great diversity around the mean.

In recent years, researchers have gained access to "longitudinal" data—that is, information on the experiences of individual students as they progress over time. This research has yielded far more precise indicators of which students are likely not to graduate. For example, while many juvenile delinquents drop out, many do not. Yet if any child has a poor attendance record in ninth grade or fails to pass ninth-grade English or math, the chances are overwhelming that he or she won't graduate, regardless of background or other experience. The research also showed much more variety among dropouts than experts imagined. Some have earned only a fraction of the credits they would need to graduate, while others drop out only a few credits shy of a diploma, largely because of outside events—a run-in with the law, say, or a family emergency requiring them to stay home with siblings. Such granular information should make it much easier to craft the right interventions for the right kids.

Yet there is still a big difference between abstract knowledge and effective practice. What do we really know about what has worked, and what has not, in schools? To answer this question, the Washington Monthly sent reporters to three large urban school districts—New York City, Philadelphia, and Portland, Oregon—that have worked strenuously in recent years to apply the new research to improve their chronically low graduation rates. The reports that have come back from the field give reason for qualified optimism. Yes, it is possible to move the needle on the dropout problem, but good intentions and effort are no guarantee of success.

Success . . . will vary according to the quality of local leaders and the engagement of local civic actors.

All three cities have taken remarkably similar approaches to the problem. Those approaches fall into two general categories: fixing existing low-performing high schools, often by breaking them into smaller schools; and creating alternative schools and programs—"multiple pathways," in the jargon of the trade—that cater to the diverse needs of those kids who are on the verge of dropping out or already have done so. All three cities also have very active civil sectors—business groups, nonprofits, local and national foundations—which are playing

central roles in the reform dramas, from spurring school officials into action to designing and running alternative programs.

And yet despite these similarities, the three cities have had
quite different outcomes. New York has achieved the most impressive progress in lowering its dropout rate. Philadelphia has
made real if less dramatic headway. Portland, on the other
hand, has seen zero measurable improvement. These results
are almost the opposite of what you'd expect. After all, New
York and Philadelphia are much bigger districts with much
higher concentrations of poverty.

Policy choices can't really explain the differences, since all
three districts tried similar approaches. Rather, the explana-
tion seems to lie in leadership and attitude. The New York
schools have had one very capable and driven chancellor, Joel
Klein, running them for eight years, whereas Philly and Portland have each gone through several superintendents, each
bringing his or her own vision. And in New York, Klein has
fostered an atmosphere of high expectations and accountability: every student is presumed capable of getting a diploma,
and schools are measured and rewarded based on that as-
sumption. In Portland, the opposite has been true. Dropouts
and at-risk kids, especially those in the city's alternative
schools, are coaxed into showing up in class, not challenged to
actually graduate, and almost no adults are held accountable
for results. (On the expectations-and-accountability front,
Philly is closer to the New York model, and so is its level of
success.)

What do these three case studies tell us about whether the
Obama administration's efforts are likely to work? For one
thing, they suggest that success, if it comes, will not be uni-
form, but will vary according to the quality of local leaders
and the engagement of local civic actors. For another, it con-
firms that school districts can get the job done and ought to
be held responsible for doing so. "The problem is too big and

complex for individual schools to handle on their own," notes education consultant Chris Sturgis. They also suggest that the administration is on the right track with the policies it's pushing, but not totally so. The vast majority of the funds the administration is making available are for turning around existing, low-performing high schools (by bringing in new leaders, new teachers, or turning them into charter schools). This is the right target, and one Washington has long neglected. But our reporting, as well as much research literature, shows that turning around chronically low-performing schools is awfully hard to pull off and will likely fail more often than it succeeds.

Any effort to lower the dropout rate must also work against the countervailing effects of growing inequality.

By contrast, the administration is putting relatively little money into the creation of alternative schools specifically for students who have dropped out or are about to. This doesn't make much sense. Yes, alternative schools can easily become dumping grounds for the hard-to-educate, as has happened in Portland. But when good systems of accountability are built in, as New York has done, alternative schools can work well and are a crucial tool in getting graduation rates up.

There are other risks to the administration's approach. On the one hand it is pushing policies to lower the dropout rate. On the other it is pressing Congress and the states to increase academic standards. Many experts warn that these are conflicting goals—that the latter will make the former harder to accomplish, and the former will create further incentives to undermine the latter. That may be true. But it's worth noting that New York hasn't succumbed to that contradiction: it has increased graduation rates and the percentage of its students who pass its high-standards Regents exam.

Any effort to lower the dropout rate must also work against the countervailing effects of growing inequality, fallout of the Great Recession, and a demographic tide that leaves more students struggling with English as a second language. Indeed, many experts think that schools and teachers cannot by themselves provide the level of social support needed to make the kind of headway we'd want against the dropout problem. Robert Balfanz, a leading scholar on dropouts and codirector of the Everyone Graduates Center at Johns Hopkins University, has put together a consortium of schools in which members of City Year, the national service program for young adults, are assigned to work one-on-one with at-risk kids to help with their studies and keep them in school. Another group, Communities in Schools, assigns social workers as case managers for students with more acute needs.

Yet even without such extra levels of social support, our three case studies suggest that real progress can be made. That finding should be inspiring, especially considering how important such progress can be to the long-term strength of America's economy and society. One study estimates that if all the students who drop out over a decade were to graduate instead, they would earn an additional $3 trillion in wages. That amount of money would do a lot to make the economic recovery that is now shakily underway sustainable in the years to come.

3

Zero-Tolerance Policies Make It Harder for At-Risk Students to Graduate

Beverly Ford

Beverly Ford is a reporter for the New England Center for Investigative Reporting.

"Zero tolerance" discipline policies became popular starting in the 1990s in an effort to make schools safer for all students and to stem a rise in school behavioral problems. But data has shown that the zealous application of these policies has led to a considerable increase in expulsions and suspensions at all levels of education. The use of expulsions and suspensions, often as a first course of action, has resulted in many older students dropping out altogether. Students who are expelled or suspended fall behind their peers and may not be able to catch up. At a time when schools are searching for ways to boost graduation rates and keep kids in school, zero tolerance policies seem especially counterproductive to the educational process.

Thousands of Massachusetts public school students were suspended during the 2009–2010 school year for smoking, skipping class, tardiness and other minor infractions under "zero tolerance" discipline policies that are creating what critics call a "cradle to prison" pipeline.

From Boston to the Berkshires, the numbers reflect a troubling trend that appears to have continued into the following school year.

Massachusetts logged more than 75,000 in-school and out-of school suspensions in the 2010–2011 school year, a study of state education data by the New England Center for Investigative Journalism has found. Details on the particulars of those suspensions is not yet available, but they do account for thousands of days of lost classroom time for students, many of whom are in danger of dropping out of school, critics say.

Topping the list was Springfield, with more than 3,000 out-of-school suspensions during the 2010–2011 school year. Boston, Lynn, Worcester and Brockton follow, each with more than 2,000. Holyoke, Fall River, Lawrence, Lowell and New Bedford each marked more than 1,000 out-of-school suspensions during the same time period.

For many observers, the numbers which raise more concern are those which reflect how much class time is lost for students punished for minor infractions.

Lost Class Time Can Drive Students to Drop Out

Statewide, students facing minor offenses lost nearly 54,000 days of classroom time during 2009–2010, the most recent year for which such detailed data about the infractions is available. The number of days lost for minor offenses exceeded the number of days lost by students charged with gun, alcohol, knife and explosive possession, sexual assault, theft and vandalism combined, the data shows.

Minor offenses are classified as "unassigned," a term used by state education officials to cover non-violent and non-criminal misdeeds, such as talking back to a teacher, swearing or truancy.

Once removed from school, many of those youngsters fall behind in their studies, primarily because a majority of students involved in serious discipline cases get no educational services once tossed from the classroom, says Nakisha Lewis, a project manager with the Schott Foundation for Public Education. The Schott Foundation is a Cambridge-based group which advocates for more equitable distribution of educational resources.

Stopping suspensions and expulsions may be difficult, especially since that cradle-to-prison pipeline begins at the earliest of ages.

The state considers school discipline a local matter, but urges school districts "to offer some type of alternative education wherever possible" for suspended or expelled students, according to state Department of Elementary and Secondary Education spokesman J.C. Considine. School districts are under no obligation to do so, however, and few actually do, education advocates say.

That philosophy has some concerned.

"We're creating what many people are calling 'dropout factories,'" noted Lewis, who has helped the Schott Foundation spearhead several studies, including one which found that students who are suspended or expelled often drop out of school, leading to juvenile delinquency, arrests and, eventually, prison. Taking kids out of class for non-violent offenses, Lewis explained, is akin to creating a cradle-to-prison pipeline.

"It doesn't take a leap of imagination to know that if you take children with problems and throw them onto the street with little or no education, we're going to breed a society of criminals," said attorney Sam Schoenfeld, of Canton, who has represented a number of expelled and suspended students. "What needs to be done is to stop this chain of events."

Even Young Children Are Not Immune to Suspensions

Yet stopping suspensions and expulsions may be difficult, especially since that cradle-to-prison pipeline begins at the earliest of ages.

According to the state data, children as young as 4 years old were excluded from school for at least one day during the 2009–2010 school year. That same year, students from pre-school to third-grade lost 1,825 classroom days because of suspensions for "unassigned," or minor, infractions. . . .

More than 2,100 students in pre-school through third-grade received suspensions during the 2009–2010 school year, 1,546 of them for violent or drug related offenses, according to Considine. An additional 574 students also received suspensions for "unassigned" misdeeds, he said.

Among those suspended during that school year was an 8-year-old Taunton boy who was tossed out of school in December 2009 and ordered to undergo psychological testing because his stick-figure drawing of a crucified Christ was considered too violent by school administrators. School officials denied that the boy's suspension had anything to do with religion and stood their ground, saying, "The incident was handled appropriately."

By the time students reach high school, suspensions and expulsions peak, especially for minority students.

A year later, in 2010, Brockton officials paid out nearly $250,000 in legal fees and settlement costs when the mother of a 6-year-old sued after her son was suspended for the alleged sexual harassment of another first-grader.

"When a child as young as 4 is suspended, something is wrong," said Barbara Best, director of foundation relations and special projects with the Children's Defense Fund in Washington, D.C. The suspensions of grade schoolers should be "a wake-up call" to school administrators that zero-tolerance discipline policies just don't work, she said.

"We don't have a child problem; we have an adult problem if we're suspending 4, 5 and 6 year olds," Best added.

Excessive Discipline Measures Can Derail a Student's Entire Life

By the time students reach high school, suspensions and expulsions peak, especially for minority students, according to John Melia, director of the Children's Law Project at Massachusetts Advocates for Children.

Melia points to the case of a Somali boy who was expelled from high school last year after he poked another student with a pencil. Despite no prior disciplinary record, the 16-year-old was cited for using the pencil as a weapon, a charge which mandated immediate expulsion under the school's code of conduct.

It wasn't until Melia, who served as the boy's lawyer, stepped into the case that the teen was allowed to return to school. He remained on probation for the rest of the school year without further problems.

Still, that incident remains a troubling reflection on what is happening in classrooms throughout the Bay State, where school administrators are tossing misbehaving youngsters out of class in the name of school safety.

Sonia Vivas knows all about that. A good student with no disciplinary record, Vivas was on track to fulfill her dream of becoming a lawyer when an encounter with two other teens sent her life into a tailspin.

Accused of stealing a cell phone and pulling a knife on a student, the 14-year-old eighth-grader was tossed out of school with little more than a cursory hearing after the mother of one of the girls complained her daughter felt threatened. For six months, Vivas, who denies the allegations, languished at home, banished from classes at her Somerville middle school where she was the only Hispanic student in the eighth-grade.

"It was pretty traumatizing," she says now, five years later. "It made me feel pretty horrible. It changed my life."

It took the intervention of a lawyer and a diagnosis of a learning disorder to finally get Vivas back to class, this time at an alternative school. Today, the Somerville high-school honors student is headed for a brighter future but the dream of a legal career she once cherished is now over, crushed by the hours spent in court fighting to get the school district to provide her with an education.

School Violence Led to Overly Punitive Discipline

In an era where the issue of school safety breeds little tolerance for student misbehavior, Vivas' story is not unique.

In fact, of the almost 1 million public school students in Massachusetts during the 2009–2010 school year, 7,075 students from pre-school to 12th-grade got tossed out of school for "unassigned," or minor, offenses alone, Considine said.

Those figures have education and child advocates concerned. "The Massachusetts law is meant to give principals the ability to make the best decisions on the spot," said Joan Meschino, director of Massachusetts Appleseed Center for Law and Justice, which advocates for systemic solutions to social justice issues. "Instead, it opens the door for them to include other offenses rather than what was originally intended. It allows them to broaden the net, sweep up at risk kids and push them out the door."

That philosophy has caused students to lose an inordinate amount of class time to school suspensions. In the 2009–2010 school year alone, Bay State students lost a total of 199,056 days to both in-school and out-of-school suspensions. In 2008–2009, that figure topped 215,000.

The reason for so much lost class time is due to strict disciplinary measures that can be traced back to the 1990s when violent street gangs began to emerge on city streets.

It wasn't until April 20, 1999 that school violence became a bloody reality when two high school seniors, Dylan Klebold and Eric Harris, walked into Columbine High School in Littleton, Colo., and massacred 12 students and a teacher before killing themselves. The murders, education advocates said, ushered in a new era of concern over school safety.

Drugs, guns, and other threatened and real school shootings have created an era of "zero-tolerance policies" in many schools.

"Suspension became the automatic response to misbehavior," said Johanna Wald, who has worked on school discipline issues for the Charles Hamilton Huston Institute for Race and Justice at Harvard Law School. Wald said drugs, guns and other threatened and real school shootings have created an era of "zero-tolerance policies" in many schools.

"Now," she added, "we are thankfully recognizing how damaging that highly punitive approach is, especially to teenagers. What they need is to be in school, to have relationships with competent adults who can steer them in the right direction."

Yet the swift suspension or expulsion of students, often for minor infractions, continues unabated even though studies show that tossing a kid out of school encourages a child to drop out altogether. And that leads to a host of other problems ranging from unemployment to criminal behavior, the Schott Foundation's Lewis said.

"Our concern is to change the process and the practices for those kids who don't commit serious offenses," noted Melia.

Path to Success Is Often Missing in Schools

"What is lacking is how to create a pipeline that makes kids successful," added Melissa Pearrow, assistant professor in the Department of Counseling and School Psychology at the University of Massachusetts in Boston. "How do we create classrooms and prepare teachers to make all students successful in school and in life? Teachers can do things to engage kids and be supportive but we need administrators to be supportive too. We need administrators to be on board."

That may soon happen thanks to two new bills currently under consideration by the state Legislature's Joint Committee on Education.

The bills, aimed at preventing kids from dropping out of school, encourage school districts to reduce their reliance on expulsion and suspension as disciplinary tactics and puts some due process rights in place for students charged with misdemeanors, according to state Sen. Sonia Chang-Diaz, co-chair of the committee. One also mandates that no student be suspended for more than a year and gives teachers and administrators discretion in how they deal with unruly students.

"We need to get students back into the educational process," said Chang-Diaz, "and we need to allow school administrators the flexibility and the authority to make decisions protecting the safety of students and staff."

Paul Andrews, director of professional development and government services for the Massachusetts Association of School Superintendents, said discipline policies need to be consistent, fair, and progressive so that punishment increases in severity with each new occurrence. School administrators also need to be able to use their own discretion to better resolve issues, he said, adding that parental involvement and support is also key.

"It requires the cooperation of local government, families and schools," he said. "We all have to work together. We all have a responsibility to make this work."

4

District Innovates to Address Dropout Problem

Michelle R. Davis

Michelle R. Davis is a contributing writer for Education Week *and a senior writer for* Education Week Digital Directions. *Her specialty is educational technology.*

The "school-to-prison pipeline" is a growing concern among educators and federal officials who worry that the high number of expulsions and suspensions in American schools is prompting teens to drop out and become vulnerable to criminal influences. The trend is especially distressing in minority communities, where African American and Hispanic students are punished at higher rates than their white peers. Some districts are choosing to address the dropout problem by offering alternative programs aimed at keeping at-risk students in school.

By any measure, the Detroit area's high-school-dropout problem is a crisis.

The Motor City area has one of the highest dropout rates in the country, which experts say contributes to the city's economic stagnation and high crime rate, and strains state and local aid programs.

The dropout rate has a heavy financial impact on the more than 30 school districts in the Detroit metropolitan area, many of which have high percentages of low-income and minority students. As students drop out and others move to sub-

Michelle R. Davis, "District Innovates to Address Dropout Problem; Cyber high school is having success re-engaging dropouts and at-risk students, earning state funds tied to enrollment," *Education Week*, Volume 29, Issue 30, April 28, 2010. Copyright © 2010 by Education Week. All rights reserved. Reprinted with permission from Education Week.

urban districts, local education budgets are slashed even further because state funding is directly tied to student enrollment.

But Westwood Cyber High School, a new online program sponsored by the 2,500-student Westwood Community School District near Detroit aimed at helping struggling students earn their diplomas in virtual classes, is having success re-engaging area dropouts and at-risk students. It is luring students from the Detroit area, and the state money tied to them, into the Westwood district.

Students at the cyber high school are often passionate about the projects they choose to work on.

"This problem is very, very serious," said Sharif M. Shakrani, the co-director of the Education Policy Center at Michigan State University in East Lansing. "When the economy was clicking on all burners a few years ago, we didn't worry about it as much, because a lot of these students could get jobs. Now that is not the case."

To help combat the dropout problem, Michigan state officials have held dropout-prevention summits, instituted a "dropout challenge" for schools, and pumped millions into school improvements, including support for online courses. With a dropout rate that Mr. Shakrani estimates at 40 percent or higher for the school districts in metropolitan Detroit, many education officials are now watching the Westwood cyber high school program closely to see if its model proves successful.

Enrollment Triples

Students at the cyber high school are often passionate about the projects they choose to work on, eager to collaborate with their peers on schoolwork, and highly self-motivated. But they are also students who in traditional schools were at risk of dropping out.

The cyber high school program uses a blend of online classes, project-based learning, and optional face-to-face support to coax once-reluctant learners to find their inner academic.

"This program addresses the dropout crisis and is a total change of a model of instruction," said Bruce Umpstead, the director of Michigan's office of educational technology. "It hits the sweet spot."

Mr. Umpstead got the idea for the program from a United Kingdom organization that created a similar program for dropouts there, and the Westwood school district agreed to launch the cyber high school program. The predominantly low-income, minority district was losing students and wanted to increase enrollment and address the dropout crisis, Mr. Umpstead said.

Westwood Cyber High was launched in February of last year [2009] with 180 students and quickly racked up a substantial waiting list. This year, 540 students are enrolled, many from surrounding districts in Michigan, a state with a strong public-school-choice program allowing students to enroll at schools outside their home districts.

All the students at the cyber high school are deemed at risk of dropping out, said Glen Taylor, the executive director of innovation and state and federal programs in the district and also the director of the cyber high school. The average age of the students is 16 1/2, and they typically arrive on the school's electronic doorstep five credits behind their peers in the educational process.

Many of the students are bright, Mr. Taylor said, but were not engaged by a traditional classroom setup.

Each student—called a "researcher" at Westwood Cyber High—is provided with a 20-inch Apple iMac desktop computer. The school also pays for home broadband connections, Mr. Taylor said.

"It was the only way to ensure access to school," he said. "If mom or dad doesn't pay the bill, then students don't have access to school, which is not acceptable."

The school, which operates year round, requires students to log on seven days a week, even if it is just for a few minutes a day. Teachers, called both "experts" and "mentors," are available to help students 24 hours a day, and sometimes late-evening hours can be the busiest, Mr. Taylor said.

Students generally work from home, but most are expected to come in to a central school building twice a week for at least an hour to work face to face with teachers and use some of the higher-level video and audio equipment available.

Each mentor is assigned six students to shepherd through the education process. The mentors work closely with their students, often one-to-one, make home visits, and oversee how their time is spent at the school. They often work part-time for the cyber high school and may have jobs as face-to-face teachers in nearby districts, Mr. Taylor said.

"Experts," who typically work full time for the school, are teachers highly qualified in a specific content area and closely involved in instruction and assessment of students in their particular subjects.

Meeting State Standards

Westwood Cyber High's educational goals aren't centered around a traditional high school curriculum. In fact, there aren't any classes, as such, Mr. Taylor said. The entire program is aimed at fulfilling state graduation requirements.

The cyber high school focuses on project-based learning.

"The only way to earn credits is to create learning artifacts that match up to the state standards," Mr. Taylor said.

All the students have real-time access to their transcripts so they can see which of the 96 state standards they have met and which are still outstanding. But the way the cyber high school students meet those standards is not through taking Algebra 1 courses, for example, or American history, or by sitting in front of their computers for a certain number of hours.

In fact, the school received a seat-time waiver from the state to take a different approach and operate based on performance, Mr. Umpstead said.

The cyber high school focuses on project-based learning. Students often choose their own projects to fulfill various aspects of high school graduation requirements. For instance, 16-year-old Ashley Jackson felt writing was her strongest area, so she created a magazine and articles on human trafficking, a subject that interested her. Through that project, she was able to satisfy English standards, writing and research standards, and some general social studies standards, said Anna J. Henning, a mentor and English expert at the school.

"We let them be really creative and explore their interests," Ms. Henning said, "but in some areas they may need more structured, prefabricated projects created by the experts."

One student satisfied some foreign-language requirements by reading and reporting on *The Stranger* by Albert Camus. Another achieved chemistry and visual arts credits for a research project on the process of dyeing hair, Ms. Henning said. Another student has already written 10 chapters of a novel about zombies.

Before enrolling at the cyber high school more than a year ago, Ms. Jackson was on the verge of dropping out. She said she had an undiagnosed learning disability and was behind in her classes.

"It was a horrible feeling, sort of embarrassing, and I didn't want to go to school," she said. "It seemed like everybody was ahead of me, and I was the one in the back of the room who didn't know anything."

At Westwood Cyber High, Ms. Jackson discovered a love of learning, and she said teacher support was critical.

"The teachers know me better, and it's a lot more interactive," she said. "I can log on to school and talk to a teacher one-on-one, which is really important to me. I feel like I have their undivided attention."

On a typical day, she logs on to do schoolwork from about 11 a.m. to 3 p.m. She said she's now on track to graduate on time.

Ms. Jackson said she had concerns at first about her social life at the cyber high school. But she found that the school offers many group projects, and that students often meet on their computer-lab days in a small building used by the district.

Though the cyber high school was launched with a grant of $300,000 from the state through the federal Enhancing Education Through Technology program, Mr. Taylor said the school appears to be sustainable by using the per-pupil payment every public school receives.

The Westwood district, which had been struggling to retain students, is now growing; it has increased enrollment by 33 percent since the cyber high school was launched.

"If you can find a district that's interested in these types of students, it's a wonderful program for them," said Mr. Umpstead from the state office of educational technology. "It enables them to care about students dropping out of our system, but it also creates an economic incentive for them to care."

5

New Report Shows Graduation Chasm for Black Males

Jamelle Bouie

Jamelle Bouie is a staff writer at The American Prospect.

A report released by the Schott Foundation for Public Education calls attention to the dismal graduation rates among black males in a study of graduation rates across the United States in the 2007–08 school year. Half of America's black male students failed to graduate from high school. The report, and others like it, is dismaying but crucial in analyzing the problem. The worst performing districts are often urban and poor, but a few surprises—such as the Newark, New Jersey, district—buck the trend and show less successful districts how to transform and reduce the black male dropout rate.

August seems to be the month for racial disparities in education. Last week, the Education Trusts released a report on the abysmal graduation rates among African American college students, and this week, the Schott Foundation for Public Education released its "50 State Report on Black Males & Education," which highlights the atrociously low high school graduation rate among African American men.

Overall, the Schott Foundation found that, for the 2007/ 2008 school year, the graduation rate for black men in the

U.S. was a dismal 47 percent. The 10 lowest performing states for black men—New York, Florida, South Carolina, Louisiana, Nebraska, Ohio, District of Columbia, Indiana, Alabama and Georgia—had an average graduation rate of 38.9 percent, compared to 65.3 percent for white men. At the bottom of the list for states was New York, with a 25 percent graduation rate for its black male students, and at the bottom of the list for counties was Pinellas County in Florida, with a dismal rate of 21 percent.

The situation is too complicated—and the achievement chasm too vast—to hold a single thing responsible for this crisis, but it suffices to say that this is a massive failure of our educational infrastructure; simply put, the majority of African American men in most states are failing to complete high school and entering adulthood without skills necessary to achieve—or even have a shot at achieving—economic success. Indeed, it's hard to understate the extent to which this is a bona fide catastrophe; high school dropouts are dramatically more likely to be unemployed or incarcerated. On average, high school dropouts will earn 37 cents for every dollar made by high school graduates, and over their lifetimes, high school dropouts will cost the United States hundreds of billions of dollars in lost wages.

Yesterday, John McWhorter sparked a long discussion of the role "black culture" plays holding back "black progress." For my part, I think these discussions are a little silly (despite my willingness to participate in them); "black culture" might be a little more cohesive than the cultures of other racial and ethnic groups in the United States, but it's certainly not mono-lithic, and the norms of an African American community in West Baltimore are different from the norms of an African American community in North Minneapolis. Put another way, "black culture" is too diffuse and too heterogeneous for it to contribute to an educational failure of this magnitude in any meaningful way.

To ameliorate this problem, we'll have to spend less time talking about some amorphous and ill-defined "culture," and more time looking for ways to repair and reform our broken institutions. There are a lot of good people doing a lot of good work on this end, but when it comes to our political dialogue as a whole, I can't say that I'm too optimistic.

6

Latinas Are Hit Hard by the Dropout Problem

Catherine Gewertz

Catherine Gewertz is an assistant editor for Education Week. *Her beats include common standards and assessment, as well as high school issues. She is a coauthor of the blog "Curriculum Matters" and also covers the states of Delaware, Maryland, New Jersey, Pennsylvania, and Virginia.*

The success of America's Latino citizens has implications for the country as a whole. Latinos are the fastest-growing segment of the population, and one in four school children will be Latino in the near future. But a recent study of the academic success of female Hispanic students indicates that Latinas lag behind their white female counterparts at nearly every level. Latina high school students are not only dropping out at a high rate, they are also much less likely to return later and earn a high school diploma. The dilemma appears to be systemic and multifaceted— language obstacles, citizenship status, economics, gender expectations, and access to high quality schools all play a part in lowering achievement gains. If the United States wants to reach President Barack Obama's stated goal of making the country a world leader in the number of college graduates, the difficulties of Latina students must be confronted head on.

Catherine Gewertz, "Report Probes Educational Challenges Facing Latinas; 'Alarming' Dropout Rates Attributed to Factors Including Stereotyping," p. 12, *Education Week*, Volume 29, Issue 2, September 2, 2009. Copyright © 2009 by Education Week. All rights reserved. Reprinted with permission from Education Week.

A potent mix of barriers including family care-taking responsibilities, poor academic preparation, and gender stereotyping leads Latina students to drop out of high school at "alarming" rates, a report released today concludes.

The study says the dismal graduation rates threaten the future stability of the fastest-growing group of female students in the nation. For the report, which paints a picture of the difficulties Latina students face as they try to complete high school, the National Women's Law Center and the Mexican American Legal Defense and Educational Fund conducted surveys, focus groups, and interviews nationwide with young Latinas and adults who work with them.

Lara Kaufmann, a senior counsel for the law center and a co-author of the study, said the organizations decided to focus on high school issues facing Latinas after a 2007 report by the law center about girls graduation rates showed particularly high dropout rates for Latinas.

"We really wanted to bring the voices of Latinas into the dialogue about high school graduation," she said.

Numbers tell a disheartening story about Latinas in public school. The reports' authors, citing a graduation-rate analysis by the Editorial Projects in Education Research Center in the 2009 edition of Education Week's Diplomas Count report, note that 59 percent of Hispanic females graduate from high school on time with a standard diploma, compared with 78 percent of non-Hispanic white females.

Black and Native American females, and black, Hispanic, and Native American males, graduate on time even less often.

Stereotypes of Latinas as "submissive underachievers and caretakers" can fuel their own low expectations.

Latinas without high school diplomas are more likely than their male counterparts to be unemployed, and earn lower wages when they do work, the report says.

Low Expectations

Researchers on the project found a big gap between Latinas educational goals and their optimism about reaching them. Eighty percent of the students, for instance, said they wanted to complete college, but one-third said they did not expect to do so.

Reasons for that outlook included factors that affect Latinos of both genders, such as poor academic preparation, limited English proficiency, instability created by immigration status, and low levels of parental involvement in school, the report says. But Latinas described challenges unique to their blend of ethnicity and gender.

Stereotypes of Latinas as "submissive underachievers and caretakers" can fuel their own low expectations, the report says, as well as those of adults at school and in their own families. One worker in an after-school program said the parents of a girl with six siblings were encouraging her to "be a dental tech or [do] something with hair." She couldn't go to college, the girl explained to the after-school worker, because her parents could afford to send only the boys in the family.

A Latina college student said her experience in high school wasn't exactly encouraging.

"Generally, academic expectations are lower," she said. "You are supposed to get married and have kids and not set high academic goals for yourself. For example, at one point when I told a teacher I was heading away to college, he said he gave me two years before I was married and pregnant."

Family care-giving responsibilities also complicate the education of Latinas.

Discrimination "both subtle and blatant" can lead Latinas to feel unwelcome at school, the report says, and they tend to be "steered away from, or opt out of, career and technical training programs in fields that lead to higher wages, but which are more commonly chosen by males."

Family Duties

A middle school counselor told the researchers that she tried to persuade an 8th grader to take a welding program, but that the girl wouldn't do it because she didn't want to risk the discomfort of being the one female in the program, only to enter the field and "earn bunk" because she was the only woman.

Family care-giving responsibilities also complicate the education of Latinas. With the nation's highest teenage birthrate, half of Latinas younger than age 20 have given birth, as well as familial expectations that they will care for older relatives and younger siblings, Latinas miss school more often than their brothers, leading to poor academic performance and disengagement from school, the study says.

Latina students also undermine their educational outcomes by not getting involved in sports and other school activities as much as their Latino peers, the researchers found. Students who are involved in such activities are more likely to avoid risky behaviors and stay in school.

The organizations suggest a long list of steps policymakers can take to address the problems of Latinas in finishing high school, including providing better child care and early-childhood and mentoring programs, comprehensive sex education, family-outreach programs, and college-readiness initiatives.

Josef Lukan, a policy analyst who focuses on high school issues at the National Council of La Raza, a Washington-based advocacy group for Hispanics, said his organization, like the reports co-authors, hopes the new federal emphasis on data systems in education will produce improved ways to track subgroups of students, such as Latinas, who face distinctive struggles.

"It would allow us to determine more-targeted approaches to helping these students," he said.

7

Pregnant and Parenting Teens Require Special Support to Stay in School

Laura Varlas

Laura Varlas writes for the "Whole Child Blog," a regular feature of ASCD, an educational leadership organization.

Female dropouts reference pregnancy as the number-one reason for leaving school. Pregnant and parenting teens often do not feel supported within their schools. This lack of support has a tremendous lifelong impact as the girls not only do not complete their own education but face difficulties in providing their children with opportunities to succeed as well. Schools need to be more focused on the perils facing this group of female students by providing comprehensive sex education aimed at preventing teen pregnancy and by supporting young parents in completing their education while coping with the uncertainties they face in raising their children.

Despite decades of decline in teen pregnancies, the United States still has the highest teen birthrate in the industrialized world. Pregnancy is also the number one reason girls drop out of school. Research shows that 3 out of 10 girls will be pregnant at least once before they turn 20. And almost half of female dropouts said becoming a parent was a factor in dropping out, according to a survey by the Bill and Melinda Gates Foundation.

Laura Varlas, "Fighting the Female Dropout Phenomenon," *Education Update*, Volume 53, Issue 12, December 2011. Copyright © 2011 by ASCD. All rights reserved. Reproduced by permission.

Female Students Penalized for Being Pregnant

In many cases schools send the message that pregnant and parenting students don't belong, says National Women's Law Center Senior Council Lara Kaufmann. Her organization works with schools to craft policies that comply with Title IX and other legislation supporting pregnant and parenting teens.

Lack of transportation and child care, extended absences and other scheduling conflicts, juggling school work and parenting responsibilities, and discrimination from school faculty create barriers to teen parents' success in school. Although Title IX calls for equal opportunities for pregnant and parenting students in schools, the mandate is enforced to varying degrees depending on local leadership. Kaufmann cites a notorious example of a school (since shut down) where students learned quilting in lieu of geometry.

Experts say that schools need to be strategic about prevention education and also provide the necessary supports to retain pregnant and parenting students.

"It's like a temporary medical condition—students should have access to accommodations like special desks, bathroom breaks, elevator use, and food," Kaufmann says. At the very least, schools should send work home to students who are absent due to pregnancy, but Kaufmann says it's amazing how many schools don't. "Do you want students coming back to school 6–8 weeks behind?" she asks.

The Pregnant and Parenting Students Access to Education Act (H.R. 2617), introduced in July 2010 by U.S. Representatives Jared Polis (D-CO) and Judy Chu (D-CA), would provide state-level grants to better target supports to this vulnerable population. In addition to policies like these, Kaufmann would like to see supports for pregnant and parenting students as part of the reauthorization of the Elementary and

Secondary Education Act. "Teen parents have a big motivation to do well in school—being able to provide for their kids," she says. "They just need the support to stick with it."

How can schools be more purposeful in helping students stick with school? Experts say that schools need to be strategic about prevention education and also provide the necessary supports to retain pregnant and parenting students.

Comprehensive Sex Education Encourages Good Decision Making in Teens

Research shows that comprehensive sex education is a proactive defense against teen pregnancy. Sex education may be a controversial topic, but most parents in the United States agree that factually and medically accurate, age-appropriate sex education is valuable.

"Poll after poll show parents support sex education that provides information about both contraception and abstinence," says Debra Hauser, executive vice president at Advocates for Youth.

Despite overwhelming evidence that comprehensive sex education works, there's a vocal minority who want to make this a moral argument, says Elizabeth Schroeder, executive director for ANSWER at Rutgers University. "But what could be more moral than teaching young people the information and skills they need to be healthy and safe now and throughout their lives?" she argues.

To support educators in providing appropriate information, ANSWER and Advocates for Youth have teamed up with the Sexuality Information and Education Council of the United States to create a set of K-12 national standards for sex education that will debut this month on their websites.

Hauser stresses that "sex education is absolutely essential, but [it alone] is not sufficient." In addition, teens need access to contraception, academic supports, connections, and hope for the future that will motivate them to use the information and services available to them.

If teens do become parents, school connections are more essential than ever in helping students feel supported.

Schroeder agrees, saying, "Teens can make healthy and good decisions, but we [as educators] have to teach them how to do that."

Schools Must Find a Way to Connect with Young Parents

Early warning signs that students are at risk for becoming pregnant aren't very different than warning signs for other at-risk behaviors, says Chris Rollison, an educator with the South Carolina Campaign to Prevent Teen Pregnancy, a nonprofit organization working with communities across the state to educate, train, and advocate about issues of teen pregnancy prevention.

Research shows that teens who became pregnant in school were often already disconnected or doing poorly in academics. "Involvement in the community and especially school is a protective factor for young people," Hauser says.

If teens do become parents, school connections are more essential than ever in helping students feel supported. "These students have some really challenging circumstances, so it's essential that they know we care about what's going on with them," says Principal Larry Jones, whose Bryant Alternative High School in Fairfax, Va., includes the Project Opportunity program that focuses on school-based supports for teen moms. "Once they know you care, then they're ready to learn."

School communities can also show students they care by allowing young people to create programs that speak to their needs. Any program targeting youth, whether it's preventive or responsive, needs to include the students' voice in its design, implementation, and evaluation, Hauser says: "For it to be sustainable, they need to own it."

Engaging students in this sort of meaningful work can further solidify their bonds to the school community. For example, when students from Iroquois Ridge High School in Oakville, Canada (outside Toronto), realized that their town was the only one in the region without a sexual health clinic, they lobbied the health department to open one.

The clinic has been open for a year, and true to the needs students expressed, it's the busiest clinic in the region. It's also the busiest because "it's the only clinic in our area where kids had a voice in creating it, and so now all the kids from the other seven high schools are using it," says Mary Tabak, a public health nurse assigned to Iroquois Ridge High School through the Halton Region Health Department. Even the name of the clinic—@232 (shorthand for the clinic's address)— came from the students, Tabak adds.

The group of kids who got this project going were not your all-stars, Tabak recalls; they were engaging in some pretty high-risk behaviors. However, they felt empowered to take up this work, and today they're all in college. "I don't know where those girls would've ended up if they didn't have something meaningful to do," Tabak says.

Educational Success Stories

Several schools provide exemplary services for pregnant and parenting students, either as part of a comprehensive high school or as a separate school or program, like New Futures High School in Albuquerque, N.Mex. At New Futures, mothers can bring their babies to school, breastfeed in class, get federal assistance checks on campus, and access an on-site health clinic and child care (both staffed by highly trained and licensed professionals).

"It's not like students come in, drop off their babies, and pick them up at the end of the day," says New Futures Principal Jinx Baskerville. Mothers bring their babies to hands-on labs where they learn about child development and parenting skills, and every morning and noon, they roll out 110 high chairs to eat breakfast and lunch with their babies.

Schools like New Futures and Bryant Alternative show that teachers play a huge part in curtailing the female dropout crisis.

New Futures isn't just about parenting, Baskerville is quick to remind. Academics, especially transitions to post-secondary education, are huge too. She cites her highly rated staff, the fact that they're adding advanced placement courses, and that all 45 of last year's graduating seniors were ready for and enrolled in college on graduation day.

Likewise, student achievement is front and center at Bryant Alternative High School, where teachers are engaged in ongoing professional learning communities about student data. Even though the professional learning communities may look a little different at Bryant Alternative—rolling admissions mean teachers must differentiate instruction and plan to meet the needs of a constantly shifting student population—the focus is still on tracking student results toward high academic standards.

Educators Play a Part in Prevention

Schools like New Futures and Bryant Alternative show that teachers play a huge part in curtailing the female dropout crisis.

"I've never had a teacher say it's not an issue," Rollison says of teen pregnancy. "It's getting them to understand that they can have a part in solving the problem." And if pregnancy prevention fails for some, schools can still do plenty to prevent pregnant girls from dropping out.

"The negative stigma of 'you made your bed'—that's no longer the case," Baskerville says. "We need to get over that and embrace, support, and respect these students."

8

LGBTQ Students Need a Safe Alternative to Thrive and Stay in School

Jorge Salazar

Jorge Salazar is a writer for College Times *based in Phoenix, Arizona.*

Harassment and bullying lead almost one-third of LGBTQ (lesbian, gay, bisexual, transgender, questioning) students to drop out of high school. These students need a learning environment free of fear and intimidation in order to complete their high school courses. Q High, a school in Arizona, seeks to do just that. The first LGBTQ high school in the state, Q High provides on-line coursework coupled with the support of volunteers and the staff of one n ten, an LGBTQ community center where students can complete their coursework. LGBTQ students are especially vulnerable to homelessness and sometimes struggle to attend school. A safe, supportive environment is vital to keeping this at-risk population from dropping out.

High school is hardly a walk in the park for most teenagers. Acne, bad fashion choices and heartbreaks plague memories of many past and present student bodies. But for some, such worries pale in comparison to the harsh reality experienced by LGBTQ (lesbian, gay, bisexual, transgender, questioning) youth in the American public school system.

Almost a third of LGBTQ students drop out of high school because of harassment related to their sexual orientation, according to research by the American Psychological Association.

A Valley [the Phoenix, Arizona, metropolitan area] organization made it its mission to provide such students an environment through which they can experience the highs and lows of high school without the added fear of homophobia and bullying.

One n ten, a nonprofit dedicated to assisting LGBTQ youth in the Valley for nearly 18 years, held a ribbon cutting ceremony on April 13 to commemorate an historic event for Arizona: the opening of Q High, the first LGBTQ high school program in the state.

Mayor Greg Stanton, along with fellow supporter Councilman Tom Simplot, praised the venture and the organization at the ceremony.

"So many kids that participate in one n ten are kids [who] have overcome incredible adversity in their own lives," Stanton said. "And this organization supports that they find the right way in some of the most difficult days of their lives so that they can provide the leadership for our city, community and state moving forward into our future."

Linda Elliott, executive director of the organization, can attest to the struggles of the youth the program strives to support.

According to Elliott, a third of the youth the center supports is comprised by dropouts, half of which are homeless. When she began her work with the organization, she decided action needed to be taken. If the LGBTQ youth that frequented the center were to have a future, they would need to get their high school diploma. Elliott knew that the youth had dropped out of school because they had been bullied and did not feel safe in a public school setting.

"They felt safe here," she said of one n ten. "They felt welcomed here. So we needed to get the school in our environment so that they would come back to school and get their degree."

Alternative Programs Offer Safety for LGBT Students

Safe isn't a feeling 16-year-old Tyler uses when describing the experience of public high school.

The androgynous youth does not want to be labeled as gay, straight or lesbian, nor as a girl or a boy. Furthermore, the LGBT teen does not want a last name printed for fear of attracting negative attention.

A self-described LGBT youth, Tyler encountered bullying issues freshman year of high school after coming out. The teen was routinely confronted and used as a subject of gossip at school, as well as prevented from accessing certain school areas by bullies.

Tyler said that being LGBT prevented school officials from being supportive or proactive in stopping the bullying, even when threats of violence had been made.

Nearly two-thirds of students surveyed said they felt unsafe in school because of the LGBT identity.

"Every time I went to them, they wouldn't do anything," the teen said. "I really think that if a straight student had come to them, it would have been different."

The bullying continued in the hallways, even after notifying school officials, culminating in a public shaming session.

"One [girl] threatened to beat me up," Tyler said. "She got in my face screaming about me being an LGBT student. It was humiliating and terrifying."

According to the Gay, Lesbian & Straight Education Network's 2009 National School Climate Survey, over 80 percent of LGBT students reported being verbally harassed and approximately 40 percent reported being physically harassed because of their sexual orientation. Nearly two-thirds of students surveyed said that they felt unsafe in school because of their LGBT identity.

When the school failed to address the bullying, Tyler began receiving threatening phone calls at home from a classmate.

"I was afraid to go to the school campus," Tyler said. "No kid should have to be scared to walk around their school."

Today, Tyler isn't afraid of hallway bullies or inattentive school officials.

As part of Q High's pilot group, the LGBT youth has found the safe school environment public school couldn't provide.

Tyler spends roughly five hours a day at the one n ten facility's classroom doing schoolwork from Tuesday to Saturday. Through Q High's online schooling program, Tyler is able to cover all the course material an Arizona public school student needs in order to graduate, thanks to a partnership with the Arizona Virtual Academy.

Tyler gets help from staff and volunteers, as well as a lunch break and recreational options just as one would in a typical high school setting. The difference lies in the environment.

"You walk into the building and there's six people saying 'hi' to you as you walk to the classroom," Tyler said. "It's so great to be in this center where everyone is so friendly and helpful."

Tyler does not regret the move from traditional schooling to one n ten's program.

"I prefer going to Q High," Tyler said. "It's a safe environment and I'm not bullied. Nobody is calling me names, and I don't need to be stressed about where I am. I can be comfortable and do my school work without distractions."

School Program Evolved from Other Activities at the LGBT Center

"We started this program so that our youth could actually get their high school diploma and have an equivalent to a diploma instead of just having a GED," said one n ten Program Coordinator Kado Stewart.

Stewart said the idea of Q High came to fruition six months ago, but that the effort to assist one n ten's youth members' scholastic achievements began earlier.

"Our youth have been telling us for the 17 years that one n ten has been around that they'd been bullied in school," she said. "A lot of them dropped out of high school or their families kick them out for being LGBTQ."

Stewart's story is similar to that of one n ten's youth visitors.

Growing up in what she calls a "tiny town" in Wisconsin, Stewart was routinely bullied during high school. Stewart said she was a target of constant harassment for being an out lesbian when she was 16 years old. Nevertheless, she started her high school's first Gay Straight Alliance and has been involved in LGBT advocacy since.

Stewart joined one n ten five years ago, starting one of the largest summer camps in the world for LGBTQ youth, Outdoors Camp.

"When I first started doing work with one n ten and with Outdoors Camp, it was really about trying to help create a safe space for other youth" she said.

Today, as a program coordinator, Stewart oversees Q High along with the rest of the one n ten staff, calling it a "big team effort."

Stewart explains that Q High is an online high school diploma completion program through Arizona Virtual Academy.

The program adheres to [the] state curriculum, like any other high school online program. The main difference is that the program is housed in the organization's downtown facility.

Critics have argued the program is a means of segregation or shielding the youth from the real world.

While the students can do their work from home, they are required to log in 25 hours of schoolwork a week. The facility is open 45 hours a week, so students can choose their own schedule and pace when it comes to their course load.

All of the work is online, as are the teachers. While they don't have physical teachers in the facility, youth and community volunteers, as well as teachers from neighboring schools, do attend the school to help students with any questions or tutoring requests.

Critics Question the Value of a Separate School

The positive mission of the program has not come without its fair share of detractors.

Stewart and Tyler said there have been arguments against an LGBT-focused school. Critics have argued the program is a means of segregation or shielding the youth from the real world.

"I know for a fact that our youth have experienced more real worlds than a lot of people have or ever will in their lives," said Stewart.

"The reason that they're here is so that they can do their math, English and geometry," she continued. "So that they can get out of high school, get their diploma and get out in the world and do whatever they want to do."

Stewart said that the perception that most people get bullied is a poor excuse not to offer an alternative school where students feel safe.

"We're not going and saying, 'You're gay so you have to come to our school,'" she said.

Stewart said the center is an alternative that provides safety, and is not solely geared toward LGBT students. Q High has straight students in its current class.

"You can come here and do boring math problems and not get beat up for it," she said.

Despite the criticism, Stewart thinks the future for Q High looks bright.

"We have 14 youth enrolled right now," Stewart said. "We've had another nine or 10 students already contact us from out in the community who want to transfer to Q High next semester."

The school will be closed for the summer, like many public high schools.

"Our capacity for the spring semester is 25, and I think we'll have that filled very quickly," said Stewart.

9

Engaging Entrepreneurial Students Is Critical to Keeping Them in School

Sylvia Watts McKinney

Sylvia Watts McKinney is executive director of the Network for Teaching Entrepreneurship (NFTE) in Philadelphia.

Several high-profile and noteworthy entrepreneurs dropped out of high school or did not attend college and went on to build successful businesses. Their accomplishments seem to send a message to potential young entrepreneurs that school is not necessary to achieve their goals. Although their achievements are laudable, these individuals are not the norm. Today's students need a relevant, rigorous education that energizes and engages them with real-world experiences on their way to graduation. A curriculum that is focused on entrepreneurship can motivate students toward completing high school and inspire a new generation of entrepreneurs fully prepared for future success.

Recent data shows that high school graduation rates have improved. But the high school dropout rate in the U.S. still stands at 8.1 percent, according to the National Center for Education Statistics. This number represents 16- to 24-year-olds who are not enrolled in school and have not earned a high school diploma or GED. And a serious problem remains:

the dropout rate skyrockets to 9.3 percent among African-American students, 17.6 percent among Latino students, and 13.2 percent among Native American students.

We've all heard the stories of successful entrepreneurs who dropped out of school, focused their energy on creating great products and services, and built empires. Just look at those who decided that college was not for them—Bill Gates, Steve Jobs, Sean John Combs, or Michael Rubin.

An entrepreneurial mindset can help at-risk students by offering them a more relevant approach to their education.

But these stories are the exception. Most successful entrepreneurs need a baseline education, and most high school dropouts lack the knowledge or experience they would need to become a future success story. Education is crucial to entrepreneurship.

Support and Relevance Are Significant Factors in High School Success

If students are engaged in school, if their lessons make sense to a world outside the classroom, if they receive coaching and support, they are more likely to finish their education and step forward confidently with their lives. A vast majority of high school dropouts say they would have stayed in school if classes were more relevant outside the classroom.

An entrepreneurial mindset can help at-risk students by offering them a more relevant approach to their education. That's exactly what we strive to impart through NFTE [Network for Teaching Entrepreneurship], and we're happy to see many of our students stay in school and grow into engaged citizens capable of building successful companies. For these reasons, fostering young entrepreneurs is crucial for the students' success as well as the success of the economy and society.

Here are some key ways to keep next-generation entrepreneurs engaged:

- Be authentic. We always stress authenticity among our NFTE volunteers. Many of our volunteers and teachers will honestly explain their personal stories: They worked for a corporation and didn't like it. They wanted to be their own boss. They wanted to control their own destiny. Students respond to that. Kids listen when their teachers are telling stories that the kids believe and that are relevant in their lives.

- Make schoolwork relevant. Students might have a dream job, but they often overlook the stepping stones to getting there. Math, science, and English classes may seem worthless at the moment, but are essential to developing life skills, which may include budgeting or crafting business plans for the budding entrepreneur. One of our goals at NFTE is to provide a new perspective connecting academics with real world applications through our volunteers. An entrepreneurial lens gives a more meaningful perspective to the work they do in school.

- Adopt students' perspective. We always ask our volunteers to put themselves in the students' seat. If teachers plan to lecture, they should expect to see fidgeting, droopy eyelids, maybe even a head down on a desk. Instead, successful teachers engage students with audio, video, interactivity, and active participation. We encourage our volunteers to become tech savvy to best relate to students.

- Make engagement a community effort. The burden of keeping kids engaged in school doesn't fall just on teachers or principals. It falls on the entire community. Our enthusiasm for education and entrepreneurship often spills out to businesspeople in the community, offering students broader support. For example, the Wharton Small Business Development Center is working with the semi-finalists in our regional business plan competition to help hone students' ideas.

- Adjust expectations. Some high school students can barely comprehend grade-level textbooks, but they've been passed from one grade to the next anyway. These low expectations can be reversed through engagement. It's only when students have real incentives to try harder that they seek the extra help they need. That's what we attempt to do through NFTE. We address all different learning styles to give every student a sense of the practical applications for their education.

Through the NFTE entrepreneurship curriculum, we are connecting academics to real world experience with very active support from our dedicated volunteers. With their real world experience and the support of the community of entrepreneurs, we're giving these kids a new lens through which to look at the world. While they're in an environment that might be saying to them that they aren't important, we believe they are. We value everyone's contribution. It's how we can make the world a better place in which to live.

10

How to Get High School Dropouts into "Recovery"?

Stacy Teicher Khadaroo

Stacy Teicher Khadaroo is a staff writer at The Christian Science Monitor.

Innovative programs across the United States are finding some success in reengaging high school dropouts. They strive to target "disconnected" youths—those not in school and not working, who are a costly burden to taxpayers.

Cydmarie Quinones dropped out of Boston's English High School in May 2011—senior year. "It was the usual boyfriend story," she says. "You put so much attention into your relationship . . . that it kind of messes up the whole school thing."

Six classes shy of the credits she needed, she thought that she could skip getting a diploma and still find a college that would train her to be a medical assistant.

"I've been doing nothin' for a whole year," Ms. Quinones says. Actually, she's been running into walls—spending hundreds of dollars on in-person and online programs that made false promises to get her a high school credential. Meanwhile, her friends graduated and went on to college, including her boyfriend. This fall, she says he told her, "'I can't have a girlfriend that didn't do nothin' in life.'" So she decided,"OK . . . I have to do it for myself and for everybody else. . . . I have to get my diploma."

Nationally, about 600,000 students drop out of high school in a given year. And more than 5.8 million 16-to-24-year-olds are "disconnected"—not in school and not working. In 2011, governmental support (such as food stamps) and lost tax revenues associated with disconnected youths cost taxpayers more than $93.7 billion, according to Measure of America, an initiative of the Social Science Research Council, a nonprofit based in New York.

"Education has become so key to getting into the labor market [that] we call dropping out 'committing economic suicide' at this point," says Kathy Hamilton, youth transitions director for the Boston Private Industry Council, which partners with the school district to run the Boston Re-Engagement Center (REC), a hub for helping dropouts like Quinones complete their education.

Dropout prevention has been in the spotlight in recent years. But increasingly, school districts are also realizing that they can do more to bring young adults back into the fold.

[Reengagement centers] offer a one-stop, personalized case-management approach—bringing together schools, private businesses, workforce-development experts, and other partners to try to reconnect young adults with a promising future.

It's called "dropout recovery," with districts deploying a host of strategies—from door-to-door searches for dropouts to alternative schools where people earn free college credits while taking their final high school courses. The efforts are taking place in dozens of cities ranging from Camden, N.J., to Alamo, Texas.

America has "long had a forgiving education system, where people can come back at any time to complete a diploma or finish a degree, but we haven't been structured to reach out and reengage youth who have dropped out," says Elizabeth Grant, chief of staff in the US Office of Elementary and Secondary Education. "As educators across the country saw more-accurate graduation and dropout numbers and recognized the size of the challenge, our school systems started to get more responsive."

The US Department of Education launched the High School Graduation Initiative in 2010 to support school districts doing dropout prevention and recovery work. Competitive grants were given out to 27 districts and two states, for a total of just under $50 million.

A personalized approach

At least 15 cities have organized stand-alone reengagement centers. They offer a one-stop, personalized case-management approach—bringing together schools, private businesses, workforce-development experts, and other partners to try to reconnect young adults with a promising future.

Since 2008, New York City's centers have reenrolled about 17,000 students, and the centers in Newark, N.J., have brought back 3,900, according to the National League of Cities.

Staff members at Boston's REC listen to each student's story, share struggles from their own school days, help them find the right school or alternative program to fit their needs, and stay in touch once they've re-enrolled.

That's what won the trust of Quinones. In November she started coming every weekday to take online credit recovery courses at the REC, a bare-bones set of offices and computer labs with inspirational posters.

In just a month—keeping normal school hours, though that's not required—Quinones finished four courses and is on track to earn her diploma in February. Although she feels "stuck" in geometry, a teacher is on hand to guide her.

"In high school, teachers never really sat with me. . . . Having teachers take out their time . . . to go through one problem for four hours, that means a lot," she says.

Dropouts are a diverse and difficult group to get across the finish line.

The REC "has expertly directed students toward options that are best suited to their needs, rather than falling into the habit of putting them back in the school where they were previously unsuccessful," says Chad d'Entremont, executive director of the Rennie Center for Education Research & Policy in Cambridge, Mass.

Since 2010, the REC has re-enrolled more than 1,300 students. About 7 out of 10 persist for at least a year. The tracking system for the total number of graduates is still being developed, but at least 160 earned their diploma within about a year, Ms. Hamilton says, and she predicts many more will do so over a longer time frame.

Dropouts are a diverse and difficult group to get across the finish line. About 1 in 5 says he or she lacks parental support, and another fifth are parents themselves, according to the 2012 High School Dropouts in America survey by Harris Interactive. Other reasons for dropping out include mental illness, the need to work, too many school absences, and uninteresting classes. Some dropouts have spent time in prison or on the streets.

Settings that offer flexible schedules and sustained personal attention are often required to help them master the skills they need.

"I'm always very honest with them: 'It's going to be tough, but it doesn't mean it's going to be impossible. And I'm going to help you envision yourself with a cap and gown a year from today, or two years from today,'" says Carolina Garcia, a dropout recovery specialist at Boston's REC.

An 'early college' approach

In Texas, an 'early college' approach to dropout recovery is gaining national attention.

At least 10 districts are motivating dropouts to come back not just to finish high school, but also to take community-college courses free of charge—sometimes enough to earn an associate's degree or a training certificate.

The most notable is the Pharr-San Juan-Alamo district (PSJA), where 90 percent of the population is Hispanic and about a third is low income.

When Daniel King became superintendent there in 2007, he faced a dropout rate of about 18 percent. Nearly half the dropouts that year were seniors—237 of them. "I felt I needed to immediately do something . . . [because] the more time that went by, the harder it would be to find them and reengage them," he says.

Former dropouts start with a college-success course that solidifies their study skills.

In a matter of weeks, he had teamed up with South Texas College to launch the College, Career, & Technology Academy (CCTA) for 18-to-26-year-olds—in leased space in a former Wal-Mart.

He put up banners around town with the message: "You didn't finish high school. Start college today." That, combined with a door-to-door search for students who had dropped out, resulted in 223 of those seniors coming back to school.

By May 2008, about 130 had earned their diplomas. To date, more than 1,000 students have graduated from CCTA, more than half of them with college credits.

Along with core academic courses, former dropouts start with a college-success course that solidifies their study skills. Then they move on to career and technical-education courses such as welding or medical terminology.

The state allows both the school district and the community college to receive per-pupil funding, so the education at CCTA is free to students. Texas is also unique in funding high school students up to age 26. (Most states stop at around 21.)

"Before I came to this school, I had zero drive in me," says CCTA student Edgar Rodriguez. He was out of school for a semester and a summer while being "reckless" and "irresponsible," he says.

At CCTA, teachers tutored him for exams that had previously stumped him. The college-success class, taught by his former English teacher, inspired him to want to pursue teaching.

During a recent visit to an elementary school, Mr. Rodriguez shared a story and Web page he had created. "I had never been on that other side of the table where I was the one giving the presentation. I loved the atmosphere," he says. "I knew then, that's what I want to do."

As a fallback, he's taken medical-billing classes. His older brother was the first in the family to graduate from high school, he says. "Now I hope to lay down the next standard of going to college," says Rodriguez, who graduated last month.

Dropout recovery has also inspired more-effective prevention. Most PSJA students now have access to college-level courses while still in high school, which keeps them motivated. And students falling behind in the regular schools can move into "transition communities" where they get more individualized attention until they catch up.

The district's dropout rate is dramatically down—from 18 percent in 2006 to just 3.1 percent in 2011. (The state average was 6.8 percent in 2011.)

Superintendent King was able to expand the early-college approach because "he made the case [that] if these [former dropouts] can go to college, why can't we do this for all students?" says Lili Allen, who is helping a network of districts replicate PSJA's approach.

"It was a smart and counterintuitive strategy," adds Ms. Allen, director of Back on Track Designs at Jobs for the Future, a nonprofit based in Boston.

11

Early Colleges Provide an Opportunity for At-Risk Students to Succeed

Tamar Lewin

Tamar Lewin is a national education reporter for The New York Times.

Early-college schools are giving at-risk students a helping hand towards a college degree while also decreasing the odds that they will drop out of high school. This relatively new educational concept—which allows students to earn their high school degree and up to two years of college credit at no cost—demonstrates that high expectations and a clear goal can make a big difference. In North Carolina, a leader in early-college schools, the dropout rate from these programs hovers near zero, while students in traditional high schools graduate at a rate of only 62 percent. Early-college programs succeed in part because they keep students engaged and provide a seamless transition from high school to college.

Precious Holt, a 12th grader with dangly earrings and a SpongeBob pillow, climbs on the yellow school bus and promptly falls asleep for the hour-plus ride to Sandhills Community College.

When the bus arrives, she checks in with a guidance counselor and heads off to a day of college classes, blending with older classmates until 4 p.m., when she and the other seniors from SandHoke Early College High School gather for the ride home.

There is a payoff for the long bus rides: The 48 SandHoke seniors are in a fast-track program that allows them to earn their high-school diploma and up to two years of college credit in five years—completely free.

Until recently, most programs like this were aimed at affluent, overachieving students—a way to keep them challenged and give them a head start on college work. But the goal is quite different at SandHoke, which enrolls only students whose parents do not have college degrees.

Here, and at North Carolina's other 70 early-college schools, the goal is to keep at-risk students in school by eliminating the divide between high school and college.

North Carolina's early-college high school students are getting slightly better grades in their college courses than their older classmates.

"We don't want the kids who will do well if you drop them in Timbuktu," said Lakisha Rice, the principal. "We want the ones who need our kind of small setting."

Notable Progress Is Seen for Early-College Students

Results have been impressive. Not all students at North Carolina's early-college high schools earn two full years of college credit before they graduate—but few drop out.

"Last year, half our early-college high schools had zero dropouts, and that's just unprecedented for North Carolina, where only 62 percent of our high school students graduate after four years," said Tony Habit, president of the North Carolina New Schools Project, the nonprofit group spearheading the state's high school reform.

In addition, North Carolina's early-college high school students are getting slightly better grades in their college courses than their older classmates.

While North Carolina leads the way in early-college high schools, the model is spreading in California, New York, Texas and elsewhere, where such schools are seen as a promising approach to reducing the high school dropout rate and increasing the share of degree holders—two major goals of the [Barack] Obama administration.

More than 200 of the schools are part of the Bill and Melinda Gates Foundation's Early College High School Initiative, and dozens of others, scattered throughout the nation, have sprung up as projects of individual school districts.

"As a nation, we just can't afford to have students spending four years or more getting through high school, when we all know senior year is a waste," said Hilary Pennington of the Gates Foundation, "then having this swirl between high school and college, when a lot more students get lost, then a two-year degree that takes three or four years, if the student ever completes it at all."

Early-College Programs Remove Many Obstacles Faced by At-Risk Students

Most of the early college high schools are on college campuses, but some stand alone. Some are four years, some five. Most serve a low-income student body that is largely black or Latino. But all are small, and all offer free college credits as part of the high school program.

"In 27 years as a college president, this is just about the most exciting thing I've been involved in," said John R. Dempsey, the president of Sandhills. "We picked these kids out of eighth grade, kids who were academically representative at a school with very low performance. We didn't cherry-pick them. Their performance has been so startling that you see what high expectations can do."

Initially, the prospect of two years of college at no cost was less appealing to Ms. Holt than to her mother, Simone Dean, an Army mechanic at nearby Fort Bragg.

"I didn't want to do it, because my middle school friends weren't applying," Ms. Holt said. "I cried, but my mother made me do it."

The early-college high schools accelerate students so that they arrive in college needing less of the remedial work that stalls so many low-income and first-generation students.

"The first year, I didn't like it, because my friends at the regular high school were having pep rallies and actual fun, while I had all this homework. But when I look back at my middle school friends, I see how many of them got pregnant or do drugs or dropped out. And now I'm excited, because I'm a year ahead."

Because most of the nation's early-college high schools are still new, it is too soon to say whether strapped states will be impressed enough to justify the extra costs of college tuition, college textbooks and academic support.

A recent report from Jobs for the Future, a nonprofit group that is coordinating the Gates initiative, found that in 2008, the early-college schools that had been open for more than four years had a high school graduation rate of 92 percent— and 4 out of 10 graduates had earned at least a year of college credit.

With a careful sequence of courses, including ninth-grade algebra, and attention to skills like note-taking, the early-college high schools accelerate students so that they arrive in college needing less of the remedial work that stalls so many low-income and first-generation students. "When we put kids on a college campus, we see them change totally, because they're integrated with college students, and they don't want to look immature," said Michael Webb, associate vice president of Jobs for the Future.

Early-College Programs Can Work for a Variety of Students

The first early-college high schools—Bard College at Simon's Rock, a residential private liberal-arts college in Great Barrington, Mass., and Bard High School Early College, a public school in New York City—were selective schools intended to cure the boredom that afflicts many talented high school students.

"The philosophy behind the school was that the last two years of high school are not engaging, and we would set up something that would make them intellectually exciting," said Ray Peterson, the principal of Bard High School Early College.

But at the City University of New York's early-college schools, the emphasis is less on preventing the senior slump than on aligning high school with college.

"Our students are actually planning for college-level coursework from their first day in the school," said Cass Conrad, executive director for school support and development at CUNY, which has a dozen early-college high schools. "And their teachers plan backwards from college, to make sure they'll know what they need to be successful in college-level classes."

Early-College Students Have Higher Aspirations

In the pine woods of North Carolina, SandHoke students start in a small Hoke County school down the road from a turkey-processing plant, and begin traveling to the Sandhills campus, nestled among the golf courses of Moore County, only as seniors. Their first college class, in 10th grade, is a user-friendly communications course taught by Cathleen Kruska, a high-energy teacher who had them discussing job interviews, learning which kinds of questions are legally permissible and doing mock interviews.

Ms. Kruska teaches the same course to college students at Sandhills, and said the only difference was that the high school students were needier.

These days, aspirations run high. Ms. Holt, for example, is aiming for medical school. She was disappointed last semester to get three B's and two A's.

"That's not what I was hoping for," she said, "and I'm going to work harder this semester."

Her high standards have affected the whole family.

"My 13-year-old is going to apply to SandHoke for next year," Ms. Dean said. "And I'm actually learning from Precious. When I'm done with the military, I want to get my degree."

12

America Should Emulate Other Countries in Addressing the Dropout Crisis

Nancy Hoffman

Nancy Hoffman is a vice president and senior adviser at Jobs for the Future, located in Boston, where she focuses on state policy, higher education, and the transition to postsecondary education.

The United States may want to emulate its northern European and Australian peers when it comes to lowering its high school dropout rate. While the reasons students drop out are similar among these regions, the methods and tactics used to find a solution are different. A practice that is common among nations with low high school dropout rates is to transition much more seamlessly between schooling and entry into the workforce, and to provide youth incentives and financial support that encourage them to continue their learning or obtain vocational training. In many countries, official school is required only until the age of fifteen or sixteen. Older teens begin a "learning to work" phase that can last through their early twenties and ends with the youth having gained solid work experience from which to launch a career. America's "college for all" approach neglects the reality of what some students need. A more targeted plan for these students can combat both high dropout and high unemployment rates.

Nancy Hoffman, "Keeping Youths in School: An International Perspective," *Phi Delta Kappan*, Vol. 92, No. 5, February 2011. Reprinted with permission of Phi Delta Kappa International, www.pdkintl.org. All rights reserved.

The United States is not alone in confronting the challenge and frustration of not being able to ensure that every student completes high school. All of the countries belonging to the Organisation for Economic Co-operation and Development (OECD) have a group of "youths left behind." These are the young people who don't complete upper secondary. Often, they're members of immigrant or minority groups, or they live in rural areas.

However, there are important differences in the way the U.S. tackles the dropout challenge and what occurs in other OECD nations. Perhaps, in learning more about how other nations address the issue, the United States can discover ideas that would also work here.

According to *Jobs for Youth*, a 16-country OECD study of transitions from school to employment, three-fourths of young left-behinds were already far removed from the labor market, either because they had been unemployed for more than a year or because they didn't seek a job. In the United States, this is a large group because of the sheer size of the population, and because the U.S. youth cohort is declining in numbers more slowly than in most European countries. During the current recession, this group will account for much of the rising youth unemployment, and it will grow as more youths experience longer periods of unemployment after leaving education. . . .

The analyses of why students drop out are remarkably similar across countries, but there are dramatic differences among countries in rates of dropping out and in solutions.

In winter 2009, at an international workshop at the OECD offices in Paris, a number of countries presented their approaches to stemming their dropout rates. The Netherlands, with a low but still worrisome noncompletion rate of 11%, described a comprehensive campaign to recapture dropouts—literally: A bus picks them up from the streets of Amsterdam and takes them to their programs. For struggling adolescents in danger of not completing upper secondary school, Norway (12%) shortened the vocational education structure from three or four years to a two-year integrated work and learning program.

Even Korea, which has a high secondary completion rate (above 90%) and has a higher education completion rate that is second among the OECD countries only to Canada, asked for help with its small dropout problem. Korea is actually attempting to *discourage* so many young people from going on to postsecondary education, instead touting the virtues of strong vocational and technical high school programs.

The analyses of *why* students drop out are remarkably similar across countries, but there are dramatic differences among countries in rates of dropping out and in solutions. Even definitions of *dropout* are a challenge: Some countries count as dropouts young people who don't complete a school-leaving certificate, others focus on a group labeled "NEET"—neither in education nor employment or training.

Caution is required in comparing U.S. high schools with upper secondary schools. In many OECD countries, compulsory schooling ends at age 14 or 15; upper secondary schools are separate institutions serving 16- to 19-year-olds. The completion of these vocational programs is more like earning an associate's degree than a high school diploma, and their academic programs are more like one year of college.

One way to avoid the problem of definitions is simply to ask which countries have kept the highest percentages of young people in school and transitioned them most successfully from schooling to work.

The United States had a youth unemployment rate in 2008 of about 11%, while the OECD average was 14.4%. By July 2010, the U.S. rate had risen to about 19.1%, and it is continuing to rise. During that year, Australia, Austria, Canada, Denmark, Germany, Japan, Korea, the Netherlands, Norway, and Switzerland (lowest at 4.5% in March 2010) were doing substantially better. Those countries had lower rates to begin with and smaller than average increases.

Vocational Education and Training

What policies and practices stand out in the countries that have the fewest young people in danger of being left behind either in school completion or access to jobs? Countries showing the most resilience to youth unemployment educate the majority of their teenagers in a mix of school-based and company-based vocational training. And they come to vocational education and training (VET) with a different purpose than we do in the United States.

Better-performing countries structure combinations of work and learning to address specifically the needs of struggling young people.

With its "college for all" mantra, the United States uses VET (career and technical training in the U.S.) mainly to engage unmotivated students and introduce them to various career options. This strategy makes the United States an outlier. In the more successful countries, VET has little to do with engaging unmotivated students, though that is one robust outcome, nor with keeping them from dropping out, though completion rates are high and pathways from VET to tertiary education and training are increasingly available and encouraged. These countries have expanded VET from its earlier guild, handcraft, and blue-collar focus to include white-collar occupations and those requiring sophisticated technical skills. VET also prepares young people for citizenship and lifelong learning. Completion of a VET program certifies that the young person has the nationally standardized qualifications for their chosen occupation.

The decisive factors in Austria, Denmark, Germany, Netherlands, Norway, and Switzerland—the highest performers—are that these countries:

- Have VET systems that serve a large number of students;

- Match education closely to labor market needs by combining work and learning in VET programs that lead either to jobs or to postsecondary education in applied learning institutions and then to jobs; and

- Have standardized qualifications developed with participation and buy-in by employers and unions that are accepted as trusted currency in the labor market.

VET programs aren't designed to cure at-risk youths of their potential for disconnection or dropping out. Although there are exceptions, the better-performing countries structure combinations of work and learning to address specifically the needs of struggling young people. Approaches include:

- Youth guarantees. The notion of a youth guarantee is gaining popularity as governments struggle to protect young people from the economic downturn. The European Union is working to create a youth guarantee that will ensure a job, apprenticeship, or other education option to young people under the age of 25 years within six months after they've left the labor market or school. From 2010, this entitlement will be provided after four months and includes income supports. Australia, the United Kingdom, Norway, the Netherlands, and New Zealand have variants of such policies.

- Mutual obligation policies. Also called "activation policies," these entail "mutual obligation" agreements among young people, their families, and the state. Young people must actively seek work or be in a combination of work and school in exchange for targeted actions to help them. In some countries, young people put their income supports in jeopardy if they refuse education or work.

- Adapted work and learning programs. Where VET is the standard pathway for young people not headed for academic and research careers, it entails a return on employers' investments, including the chance to get to know, train, and hire the young people most suited to their enterprises. To serve at-risk youths, countries alter and adapt standard VET policies and add incentives for employer participation.

Comparing Countries with Low Dropout Rates

Following are profiles of three countries—Norway, the Netherlands, and Australia—that are implementing versions of the above policies. Norway and the Netherlands have low dropout rates and a focus on equity. Australia is included because it has challenges similar to those in the United States.

An example of targeted supports is the Netherlands long-standing practice of providing additional per pupil funding to schools taking students with disadvantages.

When comparing these countries to the United States, keep in mind the size of both their total populations and their immigrant populations: Their populations make them comparable to some U.S. states. For example, both Texas and Australia have over 20 million people, and the Netherlands has the same population as Florida (17 million). Second, they are homes to immigrants: Norway has an immigrant population of about 10%, and 25% of the Oslo population is foreign born. The Netherlands has an immigrant population of about 20%, and Australia has an immigrant population of 25%.

Norway, the Netherlands, and Australia also have both universal and targeted social and financial supports. For example, all Dutch families receive child support for children up to age 18; this monthly payment can go for books and school expenses not paid for by government means-tested scholarships and loans. Those over 18 receive monthly support directly, with a larger amount for those not living at home. Norway and Australia have variants of these policies.

An example of targeted supports is the Netherlands longstanding practice of providing additional per pupil funding to schools taking students with disadvantages. Norway has put in place various language support measures, including the right to "adapted language teaching" and extra financial resources for schools with high proportions of immigrant students in need of special language support.

Norway Emphasizes Skills for Work and Life

In Norway, all youths below age 25 have the right to three years of free upper secondary education to be completed before age 24. Unemployed youths who aren't enrolled in education have the right to a job or to participate in employment programs. The guarantee is not a legal right but is advanced as a promise to young people. To ensure that the guarantee is operational, all counties must track and provide individualized counseling for youths between ages 16 and 21 who are outside of education and employment. Each county must create an individual program for each youth and coordinate that program with other social service agencies. With a low NEET rate and a healthy economy, Norway can afford such personalized services, which are especially important given that many young people live in isolated rural communities where finding options outside of school or an apprenticeship position is challenging.

For students struggling with school, Norway recently implemented a shorter upper secondary VET program: two years of integrated work and learning, rather than the standard two years of school-based learning, followed by one to two years of apprenticeship in a firm. While students must still complete the usual general education courses in Norwegian, math, and social sciences, these three subjects have been redesigned to be vocationally oriented. Early data show that the students in the combined work-study, shorter-cycle VET program are advancing in substantial numbers to complete the more rigorous and longer apprenticeship training.

[In the Netherlands,] a combination of incentives, rewards, and programmatic initiatives are keeping an impressive number of young people in school through the completion of a qualification.

Building on what it has learned about dropout prevention, Norway has introduced a new subject in lower secondary education for all young people: "working life skills." The country also has made the entire curriculum more practical.

A Multipronged Approach in the Netherlands

In 2002, the Netherlands set a goal to cut the dropout rate in half by 2011, from 70,000 each year to 35,000. To achieve this objective, the Ministry of Education, Culture, and Science made individual covenants with municipalities and schools in 39 regions for the years 2008–11. By 2009, the number of dropouts had been reduced 20% compared with the 2005–06 school year, to 42,000.

To achieve this success, the Netherlands mounted an aggressive, multipronged "blitz" on dropouts, with a goal not only to return them to school but also to transition them into a career. The Youth Care Act of 2005 adopted three strategies for reducing youth unemployment, which is already among the lowest in Europe:

- Prevent early leaving and ensure that young people obtain a basic qualification;

- Pursue an active approach to structural youth unemployment, combined with compulsory working and learning programs; and

- Conduct intensive supervision and development programs ("pilot projects to study the behavior of work-shy youngsters") as well as implement a system for tracking every student's school participation on a daily basis.

Based on these principles, a combination of incentives, rewards, and programmatic initiatives are keeping an impressive number of young people in school through the completion of a qualification. As of fall 2008, the school-leaving age was extended from 16 to 18. And in 2009, the Investment in Youth Act mandated that young people who haven't obtained an upper secondary diploma by age 18 must be in a full-time or part-time education program or be in a job, or a combination of both. Those age 18 to 27 who haven't completed an upper secondary qualification must enroll in a work/study activity. A young person who rejects such an offer can lose his or her income supports.

All students are tracked by a unique Education Number linked to demographic, employment, and benefit information; the data are detailed enough to locate dropouts by neighborhood. A Digital Absence Portal records standardized attendance data across the country daily. Through the Kafka Brigade, an applied anthropological research method, the government engaged young people in describing the barriers and problems they encounter in getting help from the system. As a result, policy is now developed starting with the student, rather than with the system or institutions.

The Netherlands' dropout programs are based at the school and community levels. As stipulated in the National Youth Monitor, an information summary, schools must "hold truants accountable, take care of pupils with problems, introduce pupils to occupations, and see that they make a smooth transition to a follow-up programme of study." Schools receive 2,500 euros for each single reduction in the total number of dropouts from the previous year, up to a total of 250 million euros for the country. The local authorities serve as partners to schools enforcing the Compulsory Education Act and seeing that Dropout Registration and Coordination Centres provide appropriate services and cooperate with Debt Assistance and Addiction Care providers. In response to data that young people want and need more work-based options and better counseling, the government has established a system to accredit the prior learning of 18- to 23-year-olds, and it has engaged large employers in helping 20,000 young people gain basic qualifications.

Australia Ensures Students Are "Learning or Earning"

While Australia has a high rate of postsecondary completion, it also has a dropout rate from upper secondary school of over 25%. This bifurcated attainment pattern means that Australia must struggle to improve the chances for youths left behind, a large proportion of whom are aboriginal peoples living in impoverished and isolated rural areas. Because Australia has a robust youth labor market, with 47% of 15- to 19-year-olds holding some kind of job, and a relatively low youth unemployment rate, there is substantial temptation for young people to leave school for low-wage jobs.

In April 2009, the liberal government released a new youth strategy, titled Compact with Young Australians. Developed by the Council of Australian Governments, the policy established education and training requirements for 15- to 24-year-olds who have left or are thinking of leaving school without completing upper secondary education, "providing protection from the anticipated tighter labor market, and ensuring they would have the qualifications needed to take up the jobs as the economy recovered."

In countries with low dropout rates, preparation for a vocation is a much more important focus of education than it is in the United States.

The compact has three elements to promote skills acquisition and ensure young people are "learning or earning":

- A National Youth Participation Requirement requires all young people to participate in schooling (or an approved equivalent) to Year 10, and then participate full time (at least 25 hours per week) in education, training, or employment, or a combination of these activities, until age 17.

- An entitlement to education or training for 15- to 24-year-olds focuses on attaining Year 12 or equivalent qualifications. The education and training placements are for government-subsidized qualifications, subject to admission requirements and course availability.

- To be eligible for income support, those under age 21 must participate in education and training full time or in part-time study or training in combination with other approved activities, usually for at least 25 hours per week, until they attain Year 12 or an equivalent Certificate Level II qualification.

Beginning in January 2010, the government gave contracts to Registered Training Organizations to provide vulnerable youths with nationally recognized prevocational training, support, and assistance in preparation for an Australian apprenticeship. The program includes a minimum of 150 hours of nationally recognized, accredited prevocational training linked to an Australian Apprenticeship pathway. Following the training period, participants receive individualized, intensive job-search assistance for up to 13 weeks. Participants who gain an apprenticeship or other employment or enter further education or training receive 13 weeks of post-placement support.

Youth Need More Than Just Schooling to Succeed in Adult Life

European and Australian youths complete the portion of their education that is "all school" at around age 15 or 16. As they mature from their later teens into their 20s, they enter a period of "learning to work," which integrates school and experience in a career area and ends with a nationally recognized qualification. By their early 20s, young people enter their careers, often transitioning seamlessly from integrated work and learning into a full-time role in their apprenticeship company.

In countries with low dropout rates, preparation for a vocation is a much more important focus of education than it is in the United States. And education itself is one component of a national youth policy that includes safety nets and special initiatives. Thus, "mutual obligation" policies, while appearing punitive to Americans because the young person can be denied income support, have a different resonance when they are part of a broader social contract that takes particular care to ensure that young people are prepared for the future. Educators in these countries would say that it is responsible policy to require young people to have the minimum qualification to enter the labor market. After all, to do productive work is a fundamental human need. Work attaches citizens to the pubic world and supports the health and well-being of families and communities. It makes sense to young people to engage in learning how to do real work and to discover their inclinations and talents as a critical step in becoming an adult and entering "the working life."

Organizations to Contact

The editors have compiled the following list of organizations concerned with the issues debated in this book. The descriptions are derived from materials provided by the organizations. All have publications or information available for interested readers. The list was compiled on the date of publication of the present volume; names, addresses, phone and fax numbers, and e-mail and Internet addresses may change. Be aware that many organizations take several weeks or longer to respond to inquiries, so allow as much time as possible.

Alliance for Excellent Education
1201 Connecticut Ave. NW, Suite 901, Washington, DC 20036
(202) 828-0828 • fax: (202) 828-0821
website: www.all4ed.org

The Alliance for Excellent Education promotes high school transformation to make it possible for every child to graduate prepared for postsecondary learning and success in life. The Alliance focuses on America's six million most at-risk secondary school students—those in the lowest achievement quartile—who are most likely to leave school without a diploma or to graduate unprepared for a productive future. It publishes the biweekly newsletter *Straight A's: Public Education Policy and Progress*, along with numerous reports on issues and policy.

America's Promise Alliance
1110 Vermont Ave. NW, Suite 900, Washington, DC 20005
(202) 657-0600 • fax: (202) 657-0601
website: www.americaspromise.org

America's Promise Alliance, founded by General Colin Powell, is committed to seeing that children obtain the fundamental resources they need to succeed. The Alliance focuses on ending the high school dropout crisis and ensuring that students graduate ready for college and the twenty-first-century work-force. Its "Grad Nation" campaign, launched in 2010, is the centerpiece of these efforts.

Annie E. Casey Foundation
701 St. Paul St., Baltimore, MD   21202
(410) 547-6600 • fax: (410) 547-6624
e-mail: webmail@aecf.org
website: www.aecf.org

The Annie E. Casey Foundation is a private charitable organization dedicated to helping build better futures for disadvantaged children in the United States. The primary mission of the foundation is to foster public policies, human-service reforms, and community supports that more effectively meet the needs of today's vulnerable children and families. It has launched a grade-level reading campaign that promotes the importance of learning to read by third grade, and its "Closing the Achievement Gap" series includes stories, results, and lessons the foundation has learned from seven years of education research.

Center on Reinventing Public Education (CRPE)
University of Washington Bothell, Box 358200
Seattle, WA   98195
(206) 685-2214 • fax: (206) 221-7402
e-mail: crpe@u.washington.edu
website: www.crpe.org

CRPE engages in independent research and policy analysis on a range of K-12 public education reform issues, including school choice, productivity, teachers, urban district reform, leadership, and state and federal reform. CRPE's work is based on two premises: that public schools should be measured against the goal of educating all children well, and that current institutions too often fail to achieve this goal. Their research, including *Limited Capacity at the State Level: A Threat to Future School Improvement*, published in June 2011, seeks to understand complicated problems and to design innovative and practical solutions.

Challenge Success

485 Lasuen Mall, Stanford, CA   94305-3096
e-mail: info@challengesuccess.org
website: www.challengesuccess.org

Challenge Success, a project of the Stanford University School of Education, is a research-based intervention program focused on three core areas: school reform, parent education, and youth development. It works with parents, schools, and youth to encourage development of the skills for success that are often overlooked in the current system—critical thinking, character, creativity, resilience, self-management, and engagement with learning—while lessening the impact of the high stress, pressure-without-purpose environment in which students struggle. Challenge Success features a compilation of research on its website on how narrow definitions of success adversely affect our children.

Excellence for All

2000 Pennsylvania Ave. NW, Suite 5300
Washington, DC   20006
(202) 379-1800 • fax: (202) 293-1560
e-mail: info@ncee.org
website: www.ncee.org/programs-affiliates/consortium-board
-examination

Excellence for All, a program within the National Center on Education and the Economy, strives to greatly increase the proportion of high need students who leave high school ready to do college-level work, and to greatly reduce the proportion of students who enter college unprepared and ill-equipped. Excellence for All is a curriculum, instruction, and examination program emphasizing the kinds of critical thinking skills and knowledge that colleges and employers demand.

National Center for Education Statistics (NCES)

990 K St. NW, Washington, DC   20006
(202) 502-7300
website: http://nces.ed.gov

NCES is the primary federal entity responsible for collecting and analyzing data related to education in the United States and other nations. NCES is located within the US Department of Education and the Institute of Education Sciences. It fulfills a congressional mandate to collect, collate, analyze, and report complete statistics on the condition of American education; conduct and publish reports; and review and report on education activities internationally. The NCES website contains numerous reports and search tools useful in locating specific schools and their performance data.

National Dropout Prevention Center/Network (NDPC/N)
Clemson University, 209 Martin St., Clemson, SC 29631-1555
(864) 656-2599 • fax: (864) 656-0136
e-mail: ndpc@clemson.edu
website: www.dropoutprevention.org

The National Dropout Prevention Center/Network (NDPC/N) seeks to increase high school graduation rates through research and evidenced-based solutions. Since 1987, NDPC/N has worked to improve opportunities for all young people to fully develop the academic, social, work, and healthy life skills needed to graduate from high school and lead productive lives. The organization's website includes a variety of resources for schools and families, including effective strategies for dropout prevention, model programs, and a quarterly newsletter.

Network for Teaching Entrepreneurship (NFTE)
120 Wall St., 18th Floor, New York, NY 10005
(212) 232-3333
website: www.nfte.com

NFTE provides programs that inspire young people from low-income communities to stay in school, to recognize business opportunities, and to plan for successful futures. Through its program offices located across the country, NFTE promotes entrepreneurship with initiatives such as its Bizcamp and NY Metro Youth Entrepreneurship Challenge.

Schott Foundation for Public Education
675 Massachusetts Ave., 8th Floor, Cambridge, MA   02139
(617) 876-7700 • fax: (617) 876-7702
website: www.schottfoundation.org

The Schott Foundation for Public Education's mission is to develop and strengthen a broad-based and representative movement to achieve fully resourced, quality K-12 public education. Its publications and research promote giving all children an opportunity to learn, and include their 2010 report entitled *Yes We Can: The 2010 Schott 50 State Report on Black Males in Public Education.*

Bibliography

Books

James Bellanca and Ron Brandt
21st Century Skills: Rethinking How Students Learn. Bloomington, IN: Solution Tree, 2010.

Karin Chenoweth
How It's Being Done: Urgent Lessons from Unexpected Schools. Cambridge, MA: Harvard Education Press, 2009.

Linda Darling-Hammond
The Flat World and Education: How America's Commitment to Equity Will Determine Our Future. New York: Teachers College Press, 2010.

Michelle Fine
Framing Dropouts: Notes on the Politics of an Urban High School. New York: State University of New York Press, 1991.

Frederick M. Hess
The Same Thing Over and Over: How School Reformers Get Stuck in Yesterday's Ideas. Cambridge, MA: Harvard University Press, 2010.

Caroline Hondo
Latino Dropouts in Rural America: Realities and Possibilities. New York: State University of New York Press, 2008.

Bill Milliken
The Last Dropout: Stop the Epidemic! New York: Hay House, 2007.

Charles M. Payne   *So Much Reform, So Little Change: The Persistence of Failure in Urban Schools.* Cambridge, MA: Harvard University Press, 2008.

Russell W. Rumberger   *Dropping Out: Why Students Drop Out of High School and What Can Be Done About It.* Cambridge, MA: Harvard University Press, 2011.

Bob Wise   *Raising the Grade: How High School Reform Can Save Our Youth and Our Nation.* Hoboken, New Jersey: Jossey-Bass, 2008.

Periodicals and Internet Sources

Caralee J. Adams   "Some States Prodding Students to Graduate Early," *Education Week,* January 24, 2012.

Michael Arceneaux   "Black High School Dropout Crisis Calls for New Approach," *AolNews.,* September 3, 2010. www.aolnews.com.

Tim Cavanaugh   "What's the Problem with Dropping Out?" *Reason,* March 20, 2012.

Center for Labor Market Studies   "Left Behind in America: The Nation's Dropout Crisis," *Center for Labor Market Studies Publications,* May 5, 2009. http://iris.lib.neu.edu.

Helen Coster   "Millionaire High School Dropouts," *Forbes,* January 30, 2010.

Steve Denning   "The Single Best Idea for Reforming K-12 Education," *Forbes*, September 1, 2011.

Jerry Y. Diakiw   "It's Time for a New Kind of High School," *Education Week*, May 8, 2012.

Clay Duda   "'Drop Out Factories' Decline, Nation Pushes for Graduation Benchmark," *Youth Today*, May 21, 2012.

Sarah Garland   "New York City: Big Gains in the Big Apple," *The Hechinger Report*, July 6, 2010.

Allan Golston   "Giving Every Child a Chance to Succeed," *Impatient Optimists*, June 29, 2012. www.impatient optimists.org.

Betsy Hammond   "Portland, Oregon: All the Advantages and Nothing to Show for It," *Washington Monthly*, July/August 2010.

Dale Kildee   "Cutting Dropout Rate in Our Schools Starts on Day One," *The Hill*, May 8, 2012.

Henry M. Levin and Cecilia E. Rouse   "The True Cost of High School Dropouts," *New York Times*, January 25, 2012.

Jay Mathews   "Online Course May Make Graduation Too Easy," *Washington Post*, April 21, 2012.

Amanda Paulson   "Why U.S. High School Reform Efforts Aren't Working," *Christian Science Monitor*, January 15, 2010.

Claudio Sanchez   "A High School Dropout's Midlife Hardships," *NPR*, July 28, 2011. www.npr.org.

Valerie Strauss   "Why Obama's 2020 Graduation Goal Isn't Attainable," *Washington Post*, February 15, 2011.

Greg Toppo   "To Fight 'Dropout Factories,' School Program Starts Young," *USA Today*, May 28, 2010.

Patrice Wingert   "The (Somewhat) Good and (Mostly) Bad News About High School Dropout Rates," *The Daily Beast*, June 13, 2010. wwwthedailybeast.com.

Fareed Zakaria   "When Will We Learn?" *TIME*, November 14, 2011.

Index

A

Adapted work and learning programs, 81
Advocates for Youth, 47
African American students, 37–39, 41
Allen, Lili, 69
Alliance for Excellent Education, 10–15
Alternative schools
  community schools, 8–9
  for dropouts, 19–21, 64
  Q High, pilot group, 55–58
  See also Early college approach
American Psychological Association, 53
Andrews, Paul, 30
Androgynous youth, 54
ANSWER at Rutgers University, 47
Appleseed Center for Law and Justice, 28
Arizona Virtual Academy, 55, 56
Australia, 79, 81, 87
Australian Apprenticeship pathway, 87
Austria, 79, 80, 85–87

B

Back on Track Designs, 69
Balfanz, Robert, 22
Bard High School Early College, 74
Baskerville, Jinx, 50, 51

Best, Barbara, 26–27
Bill and Melinda Gates Foundation, 9, 45, 72
Black culture concerns, 38–39
Boston Private Industry Council, 64
Boston Re-Engagement Center (REC), 64
Bouie, Jamelle, 37–39
Bryant Alternative High School, 48, 50
Bullying concerns, 53–55

C

Camus, Albert, 35
Canada, 78, 79
Chang-Diaz, Sonia, 30
Charles Hamilton Huston Institute for Race and Justice, 29
Child care needs of teens, 43
Children's Defense Fund, 26–27
Children's Law Project, 27
Christian Science Monitor (newspaper), 9
Chu, Judy, 46
College, Career, & Technology Academy (CCTA), 67–68
College entrance requirements, 7
College-readiness initiatives, 43
Columbine High School shooting, 29
Colvin, Richard Lee, 16–22
Combs, John, 60
Community schools, 8–9
Compact with Young Australians, 86

Comprehensive sex education, 43, 47–48

Compulsory Education Act, 85

Conrad, Cass, 74

Considine, J.C., 25, 26, 28

Contraception needs, 47–48

Credit recovery courses, 65

Criminal behavior concerns, 29

D

Davis, Michelle R., 31–36

Dean, Simone, 73, 75

Dempsey, John R., 72

Denmark, 79, 80

Denning, Steve, 7–8

D'Entremont, Chad, 66

Department of Counseling and School Psychology, 30

Department of Elementary and Secondary Education, 25

Digital Absence Portal, 84

Discrimination concerns, 42–43, 46

Dropout Registration and Coordination Centres, 85

Duncan, Arne, 17

E

Early college approach
  to dropout recovery, 67–69, 70–75
  helps remove obstacles, 72–74
  higher aspirations of students with, 74–75
  overview, 70–71
  student progress with, 71–72
  for a variety of students, 74

Early College High School Initiative, 72, 73

Economic Modeling Specialists, Inc., 12

Economy and graduation rates, 11–14

Editorial Projects in Education Research Center, 41

Education
  intense focus on, 7–8
  sex education, 43, 47–48
  success stories, 49–50
  vocational education and training, 79–81
  See also Schools/schooling

Education Policy Center, 32

Education Week's Diplomas Count report, 41

Elementary and Secondary Education Act, 46–47

Elliott, Linda, 53

Employment earnings, 12–13

Enhancing Education Through Technology program, 36

Entrepreneurial students
  as dropouts, 59–62
  overview, 59–60
  support for, 60–62

Everyone Graduates Center, 22

Excessive discipline, 27–28

F

Family-outreach programs, 43

Forbes (magazine), 7, 8

Ford, Beverly, 23–30

Foster care system, 18

G

Garcia, Carolina, 67

Gates, Bill, 60

Gay, Lesbian & Straight Education Network, 54–55
Gay Straight Alliance, 56
General Accounting Office, 18
Germany, 79, 80
Gewertz, Catherine, 40–44
Grade concerns, 18, 72
Graduation chasm with black students, 37–39
Graduation rates and economy, 11, 13–14
Grant, Elizabeth, 65
Great Recession, 11–12, 22, 77

H

Habit, Tony, 71
Halton Region Health Department, 49
Hamilton, Kathy, 64, 66
Harris, Eric, 29
Harvard Law School, 29
Hauser, Debra, 47–48, 49
Henning, Anna J., 35
High school dropouts, crisis
  entrepreneurial students, 59–62
  graduation chasm, 37–39
  impact on Latinas, 40–44
  innovations to address, 31–36
  introduction, 7–9
  Obama, Barack reversal of, 7–9
  overview, 31–32
  with pregnant and parenting teens, 45–51
  safe alternatives needed for LGBTQ, 52–58
  US approach to, 76–88

High school dropouts, prevention
  early college approach, 67–69, 70–75
  overview, 63–65
  recovery opportunities, 63–69
  reengagement centers, 65–67
High school dropouts, rates
  economic recession and, 11–12
  employment earnings and, 12–13
  graduation rates and, 11, 13–14
  improvements to high schools and, 14–15
  lost class time and, 24–25
  lowering of, 22
  negative affect on students, 10–15
  overview, 10–11
  problem of, 19–20
High School Graduation Initiative (2010), 65
Hispanic Americans, 41
Hoffman, Nancy, 76–88
Holt, Precious, 70–71, 73, 75

I

Iroquois Ridge High School, 49

J

Jackson, Ashley, 35–36
Japan, 79
Jobs, Steve, 60
Jobs for the Future, 73–74
Jobs for Youth study, 77
Johns Hopkins University, 22
Joint Committee on Education, 30
Jones, Larry, 48
Juvenile delinquents, 18–19

K

Kafka Brigade, 84–85
Kaufmann, Lara, 41, 46
Khadaroo, Stacy Teicher, 63–69
King, Daniel, 67
Kirp, David L., 8
Klebold, Dylan, 29
Klein, Joel, 20
Korea, 78, 79
Kruska, Cathleen, 74–75

L

Latin Americans (Latinas), drop-out problem
  early college programs and, 72
  family duties, 43–44
  graduation rates, 60
  low expectations, 42–43
  overview, 41
Lesbian, gay, bisexual, transgender, questioning students (LGBTQ)
  overview, 52–54
  programs for, 54–55
  Q High, pilot group, 55–58
  safe alternatives needed for, 52–58
  school programs, 56–58
Lewin, Tamar, 70–75
Lewis, Nakisha, 25
Lost class time, 24–25
Low-performing high schools, 19
Lukan, Josef, 43–44

M

Massachusetts Advocates for Children, 27
Massachusetts Association of School Superintendents, 30

McKinney, Sylvia Watts, 59–62
McWhorter, John, 38
Measure of America, 64
Melia, John, 27, 29
Mexican American Legal Defense and Educational Fund, 41
Michigan State University, 32
Minor offenses by students, 24–25
Mutual obligation policies, 81

N

The Nation (journal), 8
Nation at Risk report (1983), 17
National Assessment of Educational Progress (2009), 14–15
National Center for Education Statistics, 59
National Council of La Raza, 43
National League of Cities, 65
National School Climate Survey, 54–55
National Women's Law Center, 41, 46
National Youth Monitor, 85
National Youth Participation Requirement, 86
Native American students, 41
NEET rate, 78, 82
The Netherlands, 77–84
Network for Teaching Entrepreneurship (NFTE), 60–61
New England Center for Investigative Journalism, 24
New Futures High School, 49–50
New Zealand, 80
No Child Left Behind Act (2001), 7, 17
Non-violent offenses, 25

North Carolina New Schools Project, 71–72

Norway, 79, 81–83

O

Obama, Barack, dropout crisis
concern over, 16–17
financial help for, 17–18, 21, 72
juvenile delinquents and, 18–19
reversal by, 16–22

One n ten, nonprofit group, 53–56

Organisation for Economic Co-operation and Development (OECD), 77

Out-of-school suspension rates, 24

P

Parental support for dropouts, 66

Parents as learners and teachers, 8

Paulson, Amanda, 9

Pearrow, Melissa, 30

Pennington, Hilary, 72

Pharr-San Juan-Alamo district (PSJA), 67–69

Polis, Jared, 46

Poverty concerns, 18, 20

Pregnant and Parenting Students Access to Education Act, 46

Pregnant and parenting teens
comprehensive sex education for, 47–48
dropout prevention by, 50–51
educational success stories, 49–50
overview, 45
penalties for, 46–47

school connection with, 48–49
support needed for, 45–51

Price-Mitchell, Marilyn, 9

Project-based learning, 35

Project Opportunity program, 48

Psychology Today (magazine), 9

Q

Q High, pilot group, 55–58

Quinones, Cydmarie, 63–64, 65–66

R

Race to the Top program, 7, 17

Reading proficiency, 15

Reengagement centers, 65–67

Registered Training Organizations, 87

Rennie Center for Education Research & Policy, 66

Rodriguez, Edgar, 68

Rollison, Chris, 48, 50

Rubin, Michael, 60

Rutgers University, 47

S

Salazar, Jorge, 52–58

Sandhills Community College, 70

SandHoke Early College High School, 71, 74

Schoenfeld, Sam, 25

Schools/schooling
as dropout factories, 17
grade concerns, 18, 72
high pressure atmosphere of, 9
improvements to, 14–15
violence in, 28–29

See also Education; Zero-
tolerance policies
Schott Foundation for Public Edu-
cation, 25, 29, 37–38
Schroeder, Elizabeth, 47–48
Sex education, 43, 47–48
Sexual assault/harassment charges,
24, 26
Sexuality Information and Educa-
tion Council of the United
States, 47
Shakrani, Sharif M., 32
Social Science Research Council,
64
South Carolina Campaign to Pre-
vent Teen Pregnancy, 48
Standardized test scores, 7
Stanton, Greg, 53
Stewart, Kado, 56–58
The Stranger (Camus), 35
Sturgis, Chris, 21
Suspension policies and, 26–27
Switzerland, 79, 80

T

Tabak, Mary, 49
Taylor, Glen, 33–34
Teen parents, 14

U

Umpstead, Bruce, 33, 36
Unemployment concerns, 12, 29,
78–79
United Kingdom (UK), 80
United States (US) dropout crisis
adapted work and learning
programs, 81
approach to, 76–88
Australia *vs.*, 85–87

more than schooling, 87–88
mutual obligation policies, 81
the Netherlands *vs.*, 83–84
Norway *vs.*, 82–83
other countries *vs.*, 81–82
overview, 76–79
vocational education and
training, 79–81
University of Massachusetts, 30
US Bureau of Labor Statistics, 12
US Department of Education, 65
US Office of Elementary and Secondary Education, 65

V

Varlas, Laura, 45–51
Vivas, Sonia, 27–28
Vocational education and training
(VET), 79–81, 83

W

Wald, Johanna, 29
Webb, Michael, 74
Westwood Cyber High School, 32
enrollment triples at, 32–34
innovations to address, 31–36
meeting state standards, 34–36
overview, 31–32
Wharton Small Business Development Center, 62

Y

Youth Care Act (2005), 84
Youth guarantees, 80

Z

Zero-tolerance policies
as excessive discipline, 27–28

as harder for at-risk students,
23–30
lost class time and, 24–25
overview, 23–24

path to success and, 30
for school violence, 28–29
suspension policies and,
26–27

CPSIA information can be obtained
at www.ICGtesting.com
Printed in the USA
FFOW031210070513